THE RETREAT FROM RICHES

The Retreat
from Riches

Affluence and Its Enemies

PETER PASSELL AND LEONARD ROSS

Foreword by Paul A. Samuelson

The Viking Press | *New York*

239133

To James Tobin

Foreword

by Paul A. Samuelson

What is the single most frequent question I encounter when I lecture to students, businessmen, Congressional committees? There is no better way to learn what is bothering people than to chart the changes in the cry that emerges from the heart of a concerned audience.

Ten years ago, with monotonous regularity, I encountered this query: "How are we going to handle the soaring public debt?" Those burdens that were supposed to bow down the backs of Eisenhower's grandchildren were certainly bothering many of his contemporaries. Five years ago, particularly abroad, the question had changed. "Professor Samuelson, isn't it true that America's prosperity depends on Cold War expenditures and imperialistic ventures abroad?"

Today, things have changed once again. Without doubt, the burning question of the day, especially among young people, has to do with our national growth. "To William James, the bitch goddess of America was success. Isn't worship of a zooming GNP a reversion to idolatry of the golden calf?" As one earnest student put it, "To me, GNP is gross national pollution. I wish it could halve, not double."

As one who lived through the horrible days of the Great Depression, when GNP did indeed drop by half, I can testify that this is the hard way to purify the atmosphere and restore the serenity of a simple life. And yet I can sympathize with the concern now being shown about unwanted babies, unbridled population growth, the tasteless piling up of baubles. And those who ask these questions today are among the finest human beings one meets, whereas those who used to ask about the public debt were decent enough citizens, honest people who honored their contracts and kept their fences mended, but not human beings with whom you would want to share a lifeboat.

Biology, however, is too important to leave to the biologists. We need scholars like Peter Passell and Leonard Ross —young men whose hearts are on the side of the angels—to separate from the incredible nonsense that is now being written about overpopulation and doomsday the unavoidable kernel of truth. Pascal said, "The heart has its reasons which reason knows nothing of." Indeed it does. And so do astrologers and charlatans, zealots and computers. The research scientist who wins fame for himself, too often begins to sound like a race-track tout when he leaves the laboratory.

What can I be thinking about, when I recommend this present, careful audit of the costs and benefits accruing from different kinds of growth? Don't I know that a computer at MIT has revalidated for our time the curse of Malthus— that population grows in a remorseless geometric progression, while subsistence and resources grow arithmetically at best? How could I not know this?

Yes—but let me tell a story about the machine, a true

story. Long ago, there was a marvelous machine that could meet and best any man in chess. It traveled all through Europe, taking on each village champion and adding to its list of victories. Finally, it met a skeptical man of the enlightenment who looked deep into its structure. And there, curled up inside the machine, he found a little man—dwarfed, but still a man, with two eyes and one brain.

I reveal no secret when I say that curled up inside every modern computer, if only you can see him, there is a man—its programmer. Water does not rise above its own source. The theorems of a model can be no better than its axioms.

Peter Passell and Leonard Ross seek to appraise the axioms of growth and antigrowth. We can all learn from their effort.

Acknowledgments

We have drawn liberally on the research and ideas of others in composing our argument. We wish especially to acknowledge our debt to James Tobin. Large sections of our chapter on inflation are taken from James Tobin and Leonard Ross, "Living with Inflation" (*The New York Review of Books,* May 6, 1971), and were in fact written by Tobin; the basic argument—that we should meliorate the ills of inflation and attempt to live with it, in the interest of growth and full employment—is his. Changes and additions made in the current version are our responsibility, of course, not his, and the reader should not attribute such of these words and views as were not in *The New York Review of Books* article to him.

In addition, we are greatly indebted to Richard N. Cooper for the framework of the concluding portion of our chapter on the balance of payments, and for the clarity and insight of his teaching and writing on that subject.

These sources, among others, have been especially helpful: *Congress and the Nation, 1945–1964* and *1965–1968,* an extraordinarily skillful historical encyclopedia of federal legislation from which we have drawn the chronology of liberal redistributive measures; the writings of Joseph Pechman and William Nordhaus on income distribution, Marc Roberts on water pollution, and Stanley Surrey on tax incentives; the annual analyses of the federal budget, entitled *Setting National Priorities,* prepared by Charles L. Schultze and associates at the Brookings Institution; and Barry Commoner's *The Closing Circle.*

We are thankful for the time and criticism of those who have read all or part of the text or discussed our arguments with us, including Brian Abel-Smith, Stephen Breyer, Stuart Bruchey, Phillip Cagan, Richard E. Caves, Leonard Chazen, Donald I. Cutler, Jill Danzig, Cathy Danchuk, John Daum, Ronald Findlay, William Finkle, Donald Flexner, Henry Gomberg, Jeff Greenfield, Julian Hale, Mary Benet Hale, Edward K. Hamilton, Anthony Howard, Martin Jay, Mervyn Jones, Lewis Kaden, Richard Kellerman, James Kurth, Simon Lazarus, Susan Previant Lee, Lance Liebman, Raymond Lubitz, Victor Navasky, Joseph Pechman, Edmund Phelps, Samuel Popkin, Peter Reuter, Albert Sachs, Jeffrey Steingarten, Peter Townsend, Robert Triffin, Sherry Turkle, and Roberto Mangebeira Unger.

Parts of this book appeared, in different and shorter form, in the following periodicals: *The New York Review of Books, The New York Times Book Review* and *Magazine, The New Republic, Trans-action,* and *Le Monde Diplomatique.* We have been helped greatly by the critical and editorial generosity of Roger Jellinek of *The New York Times* and Robert B. Silvers of *The New York Review of Books.* Elisabeth Sifton, our editor at Viking, has reviewed the manuscript with both precision and forbearance.

For superb secretarial assistance, we are indebted to Cathy Danchuk, Virginia Woods, Sandra Brunner, and other members of Mrs. Josephine Ferrante's staff at the Columbia Law School faculty secretariat.

Contents

THE RETREAT FROM RICHES

Introduction:

The Retreat from Riches

"Wealth," wrote John Kenneth Galbraith in *The Affluent Society,* "is not without its advantages and the case to the contrary, although it has often been made, has never proved widely persuasive." * But times have changed since 1958. We have become a richer nation but not, by common agreement, a happier one. Gross national product has gone up 64 per cent; but what of gross national pleasure?

To many, there is an undeniable connection between consuming more and enjoying things less. A new generation of economists, environmentalists, and law professors gifted with advanced consciousness has pronounced its curse upon economic growth. "You could very well have stopped growing after the First World War," observed the British economist Ezra J. Mishan to a *New York Times* reporter. "There was enough technology to make life quite pleasant. Cities weren't overgrown. People weren't too avaricious. You hadn't really ruined the environment as you have now, and built up entrenched industries so you can't go back."

That, in a nutshell, is the case against growth: more is less. More automobiles, cassette recorders, and cook-in-a-pouch

* Source notes begin on page 189.

vegetables—less satisfaction in the quality of the common life.

The case sounds simple, but it is really a sheaf of complaints misleadingly wrapped as one. Antimaterialism tells us that we have so much now that more can't really make us happier, while elitism confides that mushrooming incomes for the masses can only dilute the pleasures of those on top. Ecological conservatism says that the process of growth ruins our environment and may even risk the extinction of life. Anti-imperialism warns that prosperity in the rich nations is distilled from the sweat of other countries' poor.

Consider for a moment the idea that the multiplying products of our factories bring little pleasure because they serve no real needs. This has been repeated so casually and often that it has taken on the authority of a revealed truth. Electric shoe polishers and hot-dog warmers have no function other than providing distraction for young marrieds falling out of love. Cars, barely two years old, are traded in for repackaged versions of the same model. Refrigerators make their own ice cubes and ovens clean themselves.

Actually, few Americans spend much of their money so frivolously. And the sharp contrast in living standards between the United States and the rest of the industrialized world suggests the obvious virtues of our trillion-dollar economy. The average factory worker in Great Britain, earning half the wage of his Yankee counterpart, may in many respects lead an adequate existence. But he does it living with his wife and children in a three-room apartment, often without a refrigerator. The chances are good that his family shares a bathroom at the end of the hall. There is plenty of food on his dinner table, but too much of it is starch. To save money, his annual vacation is spent at a cheap seashore hotel a hundred miles from home. His kids cannot afford to go to college or, often, even to finish school.

Of course, none of this proves that Englishmen are less happy than Americans. England may enjoy a less materialist culture than ours, and her poorly paid factory workers may be less prone to base their self-esteem on making money. To critics of growth, this cultural difference is far from accidental. Growth itself, they say, speeds up the treadmill of industrial life, creating the acquisitive values necessary to sustain it. As Mishan preaches, "The more affluent a society, the more covetous it needs to be. Keep a man covetous— 'achievement-motivated' is the approved term—and he may be kept running hard to the last day of his life."

Economic growth does require some sacrifice, since today's consumption needs to be channeled into building tomorrow's greater economic capacity. Societies in the early stages of industrial expansion—Britain, the United States, and Germany in the nineteenth century; Russia, China, and Japan in more recent times—have often stressed the will to delay gratification. Mishan writes, "Our eyes are ever on the clock and our calendars marked for weeks and months ahead. . . . This greed for the rewards of the future . . . hastens us through our brief lives . . . and cheats us of all the spaciousness of time."

A fashionable new critic of modern life, Charles Reich, links the materialist urge to Consciousness II, the submergence of the individual to the needs of the Corporate State. Materialism disciplines the factory worker or lawyer to endless boredom on the production line or in the office, and numbs him to the pain of traffic jams and half-hour lunch breaks. In the process, "economic progress destroys nature, adventure, traditions, and the local community."

Growth, indeed, has historically been associated with a tolerance for regimentation and sacrifice in the name of false gods. As recently as 1961, advocates of growth praised its virtues not in terms of added trips to the beach, senior citizens' housing, or more generous pensions, but in the shabby clichés of national purpose: beating the Russians to ICBMs, the moon, and the hearts of the Third World.

Growth, then, often reflects some unappetizing values. But for the most part it does not create those values. American materialism and German regimentation could survive decades of economic stagnation. The low-growth Eisenhower years did not wean Americans from their dependence on tangible signs of success or soften them up for an eventual change of consciousness. If, as Reich believes, Consciousness II contains the seeds of its own destruction, the agent of transformation is not growthlessness but affluence.

Even if America could remake her culture by reducing her growth rate, it is not clear that the trade would be worth making. English values, for example, are not unambiguously preferable to our own: if our treadmill is competition, theirs is the class system. Which English stereotype are we to believe: the content industrial laborer, protected against disaster by social insurance and nourished in his self-regard by a sense of tradition, or the disgruntled millworker, trapped by endless monotony and near poverty in a sooty North Country metropolis? Luckily, the question need not be answered. For better or worse, most Americans unambiguously cherish middle-class comforts. And the process of slowing growth is more likely to cause unnecessary ulcers than it is to alter our materialist values. Thanks to the enormous capacity of the U.S. economy, Americans have since World War II lived better than the English live today. But the average working-man is still far from achieving affluence. His take-home pay, after taxes, is about $110 a week. That suffices to keep the wolf from the door but it buys few real luxuries. Our typical wage earner knows quite well what to do with extra cash: he could use money for roomier housing to make the presence of his children less harassing; money for movies, restaurants, and baby sitters as an alternative to Saturday night in front of the television set; money to support aging parents under a different roof.

The *dolce vita* image of overabundance does not fit the facts: only 10 per cent of all families make $13,000 after taxes. And the durability of the myth is puzzling. Perhaps it can be explained as a creation of the people who better fit the stereotype: the relatively few Americans with lots of money to spend and little experience at spending it. America is very good to the few million assorted professionals, successful businessmen, and intermediate-rank executives who earn $20,000 or more a year. They are largely responsible for the explosive demand for foreign travel; wine and gourmet food; expensive stereos, ski, boat, and hobby equipment; second homes and third cars; etc. The media, from magazines to television, cater to upper-middle-income interests and world view simply because it is good business. "Typical" well-dressed matrons tout convenience foods from gleaming stainless steel and Formica kitchens that belong to $100,000 homes. Young moderns discuss the merits of color television sets in impossibly well-furnished dens from the same establishments. Those who can't afford all the trappings are still urged to buy as many of them as possible. The importance of this prosperous minority has become magnified so that their possessions become the representation of American success and their failings the target of pop sociologists. Unsurprisingly, the critics of prosperity are members of the same privileged classes, generalizing from the waste and ennui of wealthy suburbs to the whole nation.

Of course, it is true that every American city has neighborhoods of sprawling homes filled with tasteless furniture, gin-sotted housewives, and spoiled teen-agers. But most Americans buy tasteless furniture because it's cheap, and drink more to relieve fatigue than ennui. The obvious fact that a three-car garage or ski weeks in Switzerland cannot guarantee happiness is a less than convincing reason to deny aspirants a chance at bourgeois living.

A less charitable interpretation of upper-middle-class criticism of growth would be that the elite realizes it has more to lose than gain from the *embourgeoisement* of the United States. Wealth provides membership privileges in a rather exclusive club. And, like most clubs, the tangible and intangible benefits of membership decline as the club expands. Nature lovers grieve their loss of privacy in national parks as more people can afford to make the trip. Skiers must endure endless lift lines and reckless adolescents on busy slopes where they once schussed in peace. Hit plays sell out months in advance; opera tickets are unpurchasable; *grand cru* Burgundy prices are bid up by *nouveaux* wine enthusiasts; vacationers must wait for hours to pick up mail at the London American Express. Prosperity means that nobody wants to clean other people's homes, take care of other people's children, or grease other people's cars. Increasingly, service industries are manned by the resentful poor instead of the cheerful daughters of the working classes waiting to get married.

Intangible status losses accompany these losses in comfort and serenity. One of the virtues of a winter vacation in the

Caribbean used to be the uniqueness of sporting a tan in January. Now this sign of affluence is shared with a half million secretaries who can afford a week at the Montego Bay Holiday Inn. What is the purpose of shopping at Tiffany or Neiman-Marcus if everybody else does too?

Such are the rules of a democratic society that this loss of privilege is only rarely marshaled as an argument against growth. Rather, it is transformed into generalized *Angst* about materialist values, a concern for the environment, an enthusiasm for population control. Automobiles are cast as the villains of a physically and spiritually depleted society with no recognition of the mobility they symbolize for most Americans. Conservationists ignore the pleasure of the hoi polloi whose campfires reduce the clarity of the air and whose conversations break the awesome silence.

It would be unfair to tar all the opponents of growth as elitists securing their room at the top: fishing, swimming, and breathing are activities not confined to the rich. Economic growth has real costs that must be weighed against the benefits. Few of us are immune to the irritants of pollution linked to prosperity: river water used as a coolant by thousands of factories is dumped back, warmed and reeking with chemicals; insecticides washed off millions of farms into the national water supply threaten to make fish toxic to man; electric-power plants, garbage incinerators, and automobiles defile the air with gases, slicing years off the lives of city dwellers. It is even plausible, though not very convincing, that these side effects of prosperity have completely canceled out the benefits of further material accumulation—that a billion-dollar increase in output creates more than a billion dollars' worth of damage from extra pollution. Put another way, the argument implies that growth is an illusion. Each new kilowatt of electricity has less value than the house paint and human lungs destroyed by the accompanying smoke.

Economists do not deny the need to weigh the costs of prosperity against its benefits, but they do not believe that the solution requires a slackening of growth. Pollution, they say, comes not from growth but from our perverse system of incentives to industry. Today firms aren't charged for using the biosphere, so they poison the air and foul the water. Any resource for which no charge is made would likewise be over-used: if precious metals were free, every steam shovel could be made of platinum. Since nobody is charged for using the environment, its value is ignored. The answer is not to stop aiming for growth but to start charging for pollution. If Con Ed were forced to pay for its abuse of the air, management would learn how to clean up its own mess. If automobiles were taxed according to the content of their emissions, General Motors would find it worth while to build sweet-smelling engines. Halting growth would do far less to scrub the environment than a simple policy of making business put its money where its exhaust is.

A corollary to the environmental arguments against growth is the notion that fuel for the economic machine is finite: the more rapidly we grow, the more we hasten the day when the earth will be stripped of all usable raw materials. This natural-limit theory of growth is at the core of MIT engineer Jay Forrester's elaborate computer simulation of the world, which predicts economic collapse within a few generations. As a disciple, *The New York Times* columnist Anthony Lewis writes, "Growth is self-defeating . . . the planet cannot long sustain it. . . . To ignore that tendency, to predict that growth can go on forever, is like arguing that the earth is flat. Only the consequences are more serious."

The fallacy in this reasoning is found in the assumption that raw materials must always be used in the future as they are today: that when the last drop of oil is burned, the last truck will sputter to a halt. But the history of technology gives us every reason to believe that long before we run out of Arabian oil we will begin extracting petroleum from the vast reserves of oil-shale rocks and tar sands. And long before we run out of those reserves, cars will be powered with other sources of energy.

Appeals to faith in technical progress are more than a cheap debating technique to counter the Forrester school. The same week that the latest world-simulation publicity was being released, scientists were reporting significant breakthroughs in controlled fusion reactions. This capture of the power of the hydrogen bomb could provide all the energy the planet would need for several billion years. Less spectacular, but just as significant, the technology of substituting plentiful materials for scarce ones grows every day. Silicates made from sand replace copper and silver radio circuitry; European cattle feeds are enriched with nutrients made of natural gas converted by bacteria; mattresses are filled with polyurethane, which never was closer to a Liberian rubber tree than Bayonne, New Jersey. Technology, of course, is neither entirely benign nor entirely predictable. But it would be foolish to act on the assumption that science has nothing more to offer.

Other critics have used similar arguments to associate our economic growth with a drive for economic and political domination of the Third World. Expansion at home, they say, requires the exploitation of natural resources abroad, and simultaneously provides the wherewithal for American military adventurism. On the one hand, U.S. factories consume the irreplaceable mineral treasures of foreign lands—oil, copper, silver, phosphates, uranium, rich agricultural soils—thereby creating an economic rationale for imperialism; on the other, an ever-growing economy itself gives the United States the capacity to build the military machinery of imperialism without domestic sacrifice. This critique of growth raises two quite separate questions: is American growth dependent on foreign raw materials, and, if it is, does our consumption of these resources hurt the nations in which they are found?

The ties between growth and imports are as tenuous as the idea that resource scarcity severely limits growth. It is true that the American economy uses an increasing amount of the world's minerals, but that does not mean that we are becoming more dependent on them. Today, imports of raw materials constitute less than 1 per cent of U.S. income, and with few exceptions these materials can be obtained in North America (though at somewhat higher cost). If we were cut off from foreign supplies we could mine or synthesize our own. The increase in cost would represent a very modest fraction of GNP. For a giant economy such as ours, the technology of growth creates the option of self-sufficiency as rapidly as it generates a demand for raw materials: gasoline could be extracted from Colorado's limitless shale rock instead of the Libyan desert; nuclear-power reactors could breed most of their own fuel instead of depleting African uranium.

Of course, in the process of the expansion of world trade, American companies like Anaconda, Alcoa, and Gulf have developed private stakes in the control of foreign resources. Corporate interest can more than occasionally be translated into American foreign policy: at its bleaker moments, the U.S. State Department has been the drone of Wall Street. But economic growth itself is not the villain; on the contrary, it actually serves to weaken the rationale for imperialism. Gunboat diplomacy makes even less sense now for the United States than it did in 1906.

Nor is it true that American economic growth is inevitably injurious to the Third World. Underdeveloped countries need dollars to buy industrial products more than they need their own raw materials: Chile has more use for turbines and tractor parts than for mountains of copper ore, and the only way she can buy these goods is through trade. A slowdown in U.S. growth would mean reduced American demand for most of the products of the world's poorer nations.

Although growth implies increased trade, it does not necessarily imply the increased subjugation of foreign industries to American corporations. Indeed, as foreign economies themselves grow, in part through increased trade with the United States, their governments will be more likely to reject the paternalistic relationships of yesteryear. It is the most impoverished lands, those with the lowest trading volume, that are most thoroughly company nations. Liberia was until recently run by Firestone Tire and Rubber; but Brazil, her neofascist military government notwithstanding, plays off American against Japanese capitalists and kowtows neither to Esso nor Mitsubishi.

So far we have spoken only of the arguments against growth—the fruits of progress, it seems to us, need not be electric can openers, sulfurous rivers, and castrated banana republics. But rapid growth as a national policy has a *raison d'être* more pressing than the extension of the good life beyond Grosse Pointe. Quite simply, growth is the only way in which America will ever reduce poverty.

On the face of it, there should be an easy solution to poverty in the United States. A redistribution of only 5 per cent of national income could bring every family up to a minimum $5000 income. But as of this writing, even President Nixon's welfare-reform proposal—for a $2400 annual guarantee for a family of four—remains mired in Congress. Explicit redistribution of income is still political anathema.

Liberals like to believe that growth in public programs with broad constituencies—such as health insurance, aid to colleges and universities, federal housing programs, and public works—can accomplish indirectly the redistribution that would never be voted directly. But, for the most part, these and other government programs simply funnel money to the middle class. Federal transportation subsidies overwhelmingly aid the automobile, not the subway; farm programs sustain the squire, not the serf; urban renewal assuages the middle classes and dispossesses the poor. Federal housing programs confer twenty times as much benefit on a family earning $50,000 as on one earning $5000. National health-insurance proposals would multiply the burden of the payroll tax, heavily concentrated on the working poor.

The attraction of growth is that nobody gets to vote on the slice of its benefits saved for the poor. While the relative share of income that poor people get seems to be frozen, their incomes do keep pace with the economy. It is more lucrative to wash cars or wait on tables today than it was twenty years ago. Even allowing for inflation, the average income of the bottom tenth of the population has gone up about 55 per cent since 1950. Twenty more years of growth could do for the poor what the Congress won't do.

Growth is not a romantic goal, nor is it a military or strategic imperative. It offers at most a partial substitute for the measures which America should take to create a humane society. We do not argue for growth as an obsession or an object of heroic sacrifice, but simply as a sober undertaking for a nation in which scarcity is not, for many, a thing of the past.

I

Objections to

Growth as a Goal

1

Fouling the Nest

Not long ago I chanced to fly over a forested section of country which, in my youth, was still an unfrequented wilderness. Across it now suburbia was spreading. Below, like a fungus upon a fruit, I could see the radiating lines of transport gouged through the naked earth. From far up in the wandering air one could see the lines stretching over the horizon. They led to cities clothed in an unmoving haze of smog. From my remote, abstract position in the clouds I could gaze on all below and watch the incipient illness as it spread with all its slimy tendrils through the watershed.

—LOREN EISELEY, *The Invisible Pyramid*

When I first came here, you could see a corpse in ten feet.

—CAPTAIN DONALDSON, *reminiscing about the Potomac River*

Affluence or Apocalypse?

"In 1966," writes Richard Neuhaus, "few people could imagine an ecology movement. Barry Commoner and a handful of others were running around the country on a second-string lecture circuit teaching people how to pronounce the word ('Say, ee-kall-oe-jee') and were fairly well received as engaging, if somewhat alarmist, kooks. . . ." As late as 1968, a Brookings Institution book, *Agenda for a Nation,* could go on for 614 pages about America's leading problems without an index entry for "environment," not to mention "ecology." But today ecology needs no introduction.

> Scores of legislators who watched [a protest rally] from the three levels of balconies above heard demands outlined on ecology, surfing, the preservation of Hawaii, and the Vietnam war.
>
> —*The Honolulu Daily Advertiser*

If the ecology movement has often been comically trendy, it is also deadly serious and, perhaps, the most important and hopeful variety of reformist politics left in this country. Decades of progressive degradation of the environment had been ignored—or, more commonly, exacerbated—by the agencies of government. Palliatives had often made the problem worse. Interstate-highway construction temporarily speeded traffic but made Americans ever more dependent on the automobile. Federal subsidies paid for hundreds of local treatment plants to cut the flow of raw sewage into our waterways; but the rivers did not become much cleaner, and the treated waste itself created a new pollution hazard by fertilizing microscopic water-plant life. Pittsburgh reduced its industrial air-pollution problem with tough regulations on smokestack emissions, but permitted new pollution hazards to arise by virtually abandoning mass transit. Eventually, this record of social neglect and mishap drove conservationists, the young, and even the doyens of the Establishment to despair. As Aurelio Peccei, a Fiat executive, put it, "We have entirely lost the capacity for guiding the complexities of society: one can see signs everywhere."

To many liberals, this history was sobering but was no basis for being fatalistic. The chances for real environmental protection have always been compromised by confused planning and halfhearted financial commitments. Now that the electorate was aroused, work could begin in earnest. Surely, went the weary but plausible argument, the nation that sent a submarine under the polar icecap and a man to the moon can save Lake Erie.

A growing and well-publicized group of environmentalists challenge this common-sense assertion. They predict that a modest shuffling of priorities, a few billion dollars reassigned to antipollution or mass-transit programs, will have little effect. This pessimistic vision is a sober prophecy by respectable scientists who are convinced that we can no longer count on being bailed out by progress. The harsh realities of scarcity, they argue, make it imperative that we stop environmental problems at their source, that we slow the gluttonous engine of economic growth. Technology may work fine in outer space, but it offers scant hope of redeeming the sins we have committed against our earth-bound biosphere.

Indeed, technology has inadvertently magnified pollution while increasing economic output: deadly mercury-waste production has jumped dramatically since World War II, mostly as a consequence of the demand for chlorine. Synthetic pesticides, so effective in raising crop yields, threaten to reach man in toxic doses. The substitution of tough plastic packaging, impervious to chemical breakdown, for frailer cardboard means that litter remains intact unless somebody picks it up.

Could we, perhaps, grow without reliance on this defiling technology? Again, the new view is pessimistic. Growth, the environmentalists say, is drastically limited by the availability of resources. Man's appetite for depletable minerals is increasing so rapidly that most reserves could be exhausted within a few centuries. Fossil fuels—the coal, oil, and natural gas that provide virtually all of our energy—are being used up a thousand times faster than nature creates them. World supplies of crucial metals such as tungsten, zinc, nickel, aluminum, and lead are far from infinite; projected industrial demand can be accommodated from known reserves for less than one hundred years.

Even before we run out of raw materials or poison ourselves with alien technology, casual abuse of the environment may well trigger rapid natural changes with disastrous consequences. The world, some scientists conjecture, is speeding toward an ecological judgment day on which seemingly trivial violations of nature will threaten the existence of man. By this reasoning, to assume offhandedly that economic growth can go on forever is suicidal.

Predictions of imminent doom may be speculative, but they are even more frightening than prophecies of a more gradual end through resource exhaustion. And behind the strong language are some reasoned, scientific arguments. Ecologists tell us that the biological accident that created and continues to sustain man is only thinly defended against disaster. Carbon, oxygen, and nitrogen, critical to life, are shuttled between earth, air, and living organisms through delicate ecological chains. Almost any economic activity disrupts these chains—the bigger the scale and the more modern the organization, the more disruptive it is. Coal is burned, increasing the carbon dioxide and smoke in the air.

Insects are exterminated with pesticides, cutting off a food source for numerous higher life forms. Natural vegetation is cleared for farming, reducing the amount of oxygen released into the air, increasing the rate of moisture loss from the soil, and modifying the capacity of the land to resist erosion. Underground rivers are tapped for irrigation, lowering the water table. The consequences of these disruptions are rarely understood before major environmental changes are under way. The ecological chains are so complex and interwoven that we have only primitive knowledge of the effect of severing a link or two. A few examples culled from the list of hazards are illustrative.

Phosphorus and nitrogen compounds from modern laundry detergents, processed sewage, and fertilizers are pumped into lakes and rivers. Innocuous in themselves, these chemicals disrupt the balance of animal and vegetable life in large lakes. Colonies of microscopic algae feast on the nutrients and then die, leaving great masses of organic wastes on the lake bottoms. At unpredictable intervals, these wastes can siphon off much of the natural oxygen supply in the water. The result: rapid changes in the lake's capacity to sustain aquatic life. Lake Erie has been particularly vulnerable to this process. Some types of fish have disappeared altogether, while all fish catches are down sharply. Thanks to a doubling of plant-nutrient discharges over the past decades, other important lakes and coastal fishing waters are not far behind.

Consider another ecological snare. Every use of coal or oil to generate heat discharges the by-products of combustion into the atmosphere. Of course, the local effects are obvious to any city dweller who endures his daily measure of filth. But scientists suspect that far more subtle changes to the environment are taking place. Natural combustion creates heat, carbon dioxide, and smoke as it consumes oxygen. Atmospheric carbon dioxide, in any conceivable concentration, is harmless to any form of life, but it affects the capacity of the earth to radiate heat absorbed from the sun. The gas creates a sort of greenhouse effect in which solar energy can enter the atmosphere but is prevented from leaking back into space. By the year 2000, thanks to man's use of fossil fuels, atmospheric carbon dioxide will increase by one fifth, tending to raise the surface temperature of the earth by perhaps one degree. At the same time, however, the average level of smoke particles in the atmosphere will increase, acting as a shield against solar radiation. Thus the smoke tends to cool us, but no one knows on balance whether the earth's temperature will go up or down.

Atmospheric temperature has little direct effect on our lives—a few degrees one way or another would hardly be noticed. Yet those small changes might affect weather patterns and, in turn, change the size of the polar icecaps. A major temperature increase could melt enough ice to flood the low countries of Europe and all of the world's major harbors. A decrease could trigger a new ice age.

Similarly, the introduction of supersonic commercial aircraft will have unknown effects on the upper atmosphere. Once in operation, these SSTs will emit exhaust particles and water vapor into the stratosphere, thereby changing its natural capacity to reflect solar radiation and perhaps seriously affecting the climate. Moreover, some scientists forecast a dramatic change in the energy-filtering capacity of the stratosphere, which would permit more ultraviolet rays to reach us and thereby multiply the incidence of skin cancer.

The list of imponderable hazards can be extended further.

Modern agricultural methods permit enormous improvements in crop yields through the use of fertilizers, pesticides, and irrigation. They constitute the main weapons of the so-called "Green Revolution." Yet all of these measures threaten to defile the environment. Fertilizer washed off the soil is an important cause of stream and lake pollution; it is also a suspected threat to infants when it infiltrates drinking water. Pesticides, such as DDT, work their way through the food chain and collect in birds and animals; current, low-concentration levels have already reduced fish supplies in some areas. Major irrigation projects rarely have a benign effect on local ecologies, and occasionally have produced disaster. The Aswan dam on the Nile has induced a snail-population explosion spreading a debilitating disease to the peasants who work near the river. And all of these environmental difficulties may be just a preview of coming detractions; even if all industry were to shut down tomorrow, the impact of existing pollution would not be known for decades.

This vision of future economic growth is thus quite grim. We seem trapped in a pattern of rapidly increasing pollution and rapidly decreasing resource reserves, complicated by the omnipresent danger of ecological disaster. If history is adequate evidence to judge the future, the technology that has permitted us our economic miracles will sabotage all efforts to break out of the circle.

Given this scenario, the alternatives for avoiding collapse are very limited. Further expansion of economic output would appear intolerable; in fact, substantial contraction might be inevitable. Anthony Lewis probably speaks for most environmentalists when he writes, "The conclusion of the scientists [is that] . . . there is only one way to avoid the pattern of boom crashing into earthly limits. That is to moderate all the interconnected factors: population, pollution, industrial production. The essential is to stop economic growth."

It is difficult to quarrel with much of the environmentalists' message. Economic growth has been pursued in ignorance of the environmental costs. As a British scientists' broadside in *Ecologist Magazine* sees it: "Industrial man in the world today is like a bull in a china shop . . . [who has] set himself the goal of reducing it to rubble in the shortest possible time." By pretending that the problems don't exist, we have tempted the gods to anger. At best, we could end up waist high in pollutants without the resources to provide even the necessities. At worst, we could trigger disastrous changes in climate or earth chemistry that could make the planet unfit for human life.

But in prescribing an end to growth as the remedy, the doomsday environmentalists have made an error not so different from those who would ignore the implications of ecology altogether: the past is an uncertain measure of the future. Though growth has been associated with the rape of the biosphere for the last few centuries, this does not mean that we are powerless to sever the association. The real problem is maintaining some perspective on an issue that seems to beg for ideological commitment. To a large extent, the arguments about ecology and growth have been made at the expense of reason. Either one must agree with the environmentalists who assert that stopping growth is the key to survival, or one feels compelled to defend the idea "that conditions are getting better not worse . . . that the danger today resides in the Disaster Lobby . . . who are undermining the

American system and threatening the lives and fortunes of the American people."

The temptation to choose sides is undeniably strong: that we are close to doomsday makes little intuitive sense to the majority in a nation conditioned to a toaster-oven in every kitchen and a car in every garage; that the world can go on as it is appears equally absurd for converts to the cause. Yet should neither view turn out to be correct, the penalties of choosing either extreme will be considerable. If the alarmists are right, a policy of business as usual will mean disaster. But if they are wrong, a policy of deliberately halting economic growth would unnecessarily condemn much of the world to permanent poverty. Any remotely probable redistribution of current output would leave most of the world with an annual income of less than $500.

Perhaps the best way of presenting the case for a middle position is to examine the assumptions behind the most ambitious scenario of doom offered to date, *The Limits to Growth*, by a team of computer specialists led by Dennis Meadows. Produced under the auspices of the Club of Rome, a self-styled "invisible college" of elite international corporation executives and technocrats, this volume has caught the attention of the press with its dramatic prediction of world economic collapse within decades unless the engine of economic growth is slowed to idle.

The Limits to Growth approaches the problem of forecasting the future straightforwardly enough, employing the time-honored technique of computer-aided mathematical simulation. Simulation has proved invaluable as a device for testing engineering designs at little cost and no risk to lives. Instead of simply building a prototype aircraft and seeing if it flies, the airplane's characteristics are condensed down to a series of computer equations that simulate flight. The Apollo moon rocket made thousands of trips on an IBM machine before it was even built. Economists also use simulation, though their successes have been modest. Thanks in part to our rather crude understanding of how the economy works, simulation models have a spotty record in using current data to predict national income, unemployment, and inflation even a year or two in advance.

But *The Limits to Growth* is cast from a more heroic mold than any engineering or economic study. The Meadows team focuses its attention on the whole world, and extends its time horizon to centuries. Factors that the researchers believe influence population and income are boiled down to a few dozen equations. The crucial variables—population, industrial output, raw-materials reserves, food production, and pollution—all interact in ways that are at least superficially reasonable: population growth is limited by food output, health services, and pollution; industrial and agricultural growth are limited by resource availability and pollution. *Limits* is thus able to create a hypothetical future based on knowledge of the past.

As a first approximation of that future, the *Limits* study assumes that the world is incapable of adjusting to problems of scarcity. Technology stagnates and pollution is ignored, even as it chokes millions to death. In their grim scenario, resource scarcity, rather than environmental decay, delivers the *coup de grâce;* world reserves of vital elements (silver, tungsten, mercury, etc.) are exhausted within forty years. Around 2020, the pinch becomes tight enough to cause a fall in per-capita income. A few decades later, malnutrition and lagging health services abruptly reverse the climbing population trend. By the year 2100, the resource base has shrunk so badly that the world economy is unable to sustain even nineteenth-century living standards.

Rather than demonstrating the need to halt economic growth, the scenario only plausibly illustrates the obvious need for continued scientific progress to sustain current levels of prosperity. The quality of life in the future surely depends on the progress of technology and, to some degree, on our willingness to slow population growth. But that should come as no surprise to developed nations of the world where people are already enormously dependent on modern techniques. If the telephone company were restricted to turn-of-the-century technology, 20 million operators would be needed to handle today's volume of calls. Or, as the editor of *The Economist* put it, an extrapolation of the trends of the 1880s would show today's cities buried under horse manure.

By the same measure, the simulation provides some insight into the probable hazards of continued population growth. Large families are a luxury in the developed nations; population growth reduces the possibility of privacy for many and causes genuine hardship for those at the bottom of the economic ladder. Thanks to the new technology of birth control, the problem may be eliminated altogether without government interference. But, for the less developed countries, the population explosion may wipe out all the gains from output growth, and thereby condemn them to unending poverty.

The authors of *Limits* and many environmentalists have much more in mind than these simple lessons, however. They are out to show that pollution, malnutrition, and population growth cannot be attacked directly, but only by stopping economic growth. They argue that any reasonable modification of their assumptions to account for new technology, nonpolluting industrial processes, and population control might postpone collapse but would not avoid it. Under the most sanguine conditions imaginable, the Meadows team contends, "The limits of growth will be reached sometime within the next hundred years. The most probable result will be a rather sudden and uncontrollable decline in both population and industrial capacity." Even if technology doubled known resources and crop yields, pollution were cut by three-fourths, and birth control eliminated all accidental pregnancies, growth would turn out to be self-limiting. In no more than a century, the collective weight of food shortages, raw-material depletion, and pollution would reverse expansion. The only way to avoid collapse and its attendant miseries is to halt growth now.

It is no coincidence that all the *Limits* simulations end in collapse. A close examination of their technique reveals the weakness of the doomsday arguments. As in any simulation, the results depend on the information initially fed to the computer. And the *Limits* team fixes the wheel; no matter how many times you play, there is only one plausible outcome. Critical to the model is the notion that growth creates stresses (on the environment, on mineral and agricultural resources) which multiply geometrically. Like compound interest on a savings account, these stresses accumulate at a constantly accelerating pace: every child born is not only another mouth to feed but another potential parent, every new factory not only drains away resources but increases our capacity to build more factories. Geometric (or, as mathematicians prefer to call it, exponential) growth must eventually produce spectacular results. If the Indians who sold Manhattan three hundred years ago for $24 could have left their money untouched in a bank paying 7 per cent (a number chosen no more arbitrarily than many in *Limits*), they would have more than $25 billion today.

While the world model hypothesizes exponential growth for our future industrial and agricultural activities, it places arbitrary, nonexponential limits on the technical progress that might accommodate them. New methods of locating and mining ores, or recycling used materials, are assigned the ability to do no more than double reserve capacity; agricultural research can do no more than double land yields; pollution can cut emissions from each source by no more than three-fourths. Hence the end is inevitable. Economic demands must outstrip economic capacities simply because of the assumption of exponential growth in the former.

The basic idea is hardly new. The Reverend Thomas Malthus made a similar point two centuries ago without benefit of computer print-outs or blinking lights. Malthus argued that people tend to multiply exponentially while, at best, the food supply increases at a constant rate. He expected that starvation and war would periodically redress the balance. The cause has never been long without spokesmen. In the 1920s, John Ise recast the Malthusian dilemma in terms of natural resources; twenty years ago, the issue was resuscitated by the Truman Administration's Paley Commission report on resource scarcity.

It is true that exponential economic growth cannot go on forever if technology does not keep up or if resources are exhausted. If technology is going to fail us we might save ourselves much misery by stopping before we reach the limits, but there is no particular criterion beyond myopia on which to base that speculation. Malthus was wrong; food capacity has kept up with population. The Paley Commission was wrong; there are no signs of a general shortage of raw materials. While no one knows for certain, technical progress does not seem to be slowing down. The best econometric estimates suggest that it is indeed growing exponentially.

Not only are natural-resource reserves and technology calculated on the most conservative assumptions in *The Limits to Growth,* but the world economy is assumed to be incapable of adjusting to shortages once they appear. This is largely due to the absence of prices as a variable in the projection of how resources will be used. In the real world, rising prices act as an economic spur to conserve scarce resources, providing profit incentives to use cheaper materials in their place, stimulating private efforts to discover new ways to save on resource inputs, and making renewed exploration attempts more lucrative. In fact, natural-resource prices have remained low, giving little evidence of coming shortages; mineral prices have roughly kept pace with industrial prices for the past one hundred years. The reasons are not hard to find. Technical change has dramatically reduced exploration and extraction costs in spite of the scarcity of high-grade ores—the mining operation that took one hundred man-hours in 1929 used only forty-five in 1957. And technology continues to widen the opportunities to substitute plentiful materials for scarce ones: plastics for metal; synthetic fibers for natural; irrigated, chemically treated land for naturally fertile; etc.

Of course, nature does pose some constraint on economic output. The earth is finite, hence, in some sense, there are limits. But those limits may be so distant that they need not concern us any more than the fact that the sun will burn out someday casts a shadow on our lives. Most scientists agree that the ultimate limit must be calculated in terms of the availability of energy. In effect, energy can make up for raw-material scarcity. Given enough energy, minerals can be reclaimed from under the sea, or from sea water itself; trace minerals could be recycled from scrap or garbage. With enough energy, we could even extract minerals from other planets.

Conventional sources of energy are confined to fossil fuels (coal, oil, natural gas) and fission fuels (uranium). While supplies of these are much larger than is generally known—Canada's tar sands and Colorado's shale-rock-oil deposits dwarf the great oil reserves of the Persian Gulf—expected use rates could still exhaust them within one thousand years. However, the infant technology of nuclear fusion already shows signs of freeing us from the constraints of conventional energy sources. It is possible that nuclear-fusion reactors, in essence controlled hydrogen bombs, can provide safe, cheap, virtually limitless power within decades. The fuel for nuclear fusion is hydrogen, an element as available as sea water. No one has yet been able to generate a fusion reaction in the laboratory, let alone in a commercial power plant—the technical problems of heating hydrogen to millions of degrees within a tiny fraction of a second are staggering. But the goal now appears within reach—close enough so that at least one American corporation is developing a fusion reactor without government subsidies.

If the natural-resources-limits argument is a red herring, what of the danger of ecological disaster? Here the *Limits to Growth* simulation can offer little hard evidence. The Meadows team simply assumes that abatement practices will at best reduce pollution by three-quarters. Yet that goal could be accomplished using techniques that exist today, and it ignores the promise of innovations that are being developed.

Relatively pollution-free autos can be built if we have the political will to insist; electric power can be generated with minimal pollution if we are willing to pay a reasonable price.

This does not mean, of course, that ecological damage should be dismissed outright as the ultimate limit to growth. But in their fervor to publicize the dangers of ignoring the environment altogether, many ecologists have overstated the case. Survival may demand some modification in our behavior. However, that need not mean an end to economic growth.

Much of the recognized global ecological threat comes from known contaminants—smoke, high-altitude fuel combustion, pesticides, fertilizers—which can be attacked directly without opting for an end to economic expansion. A large portion of industrial air pollutants can be eliminated without crippling production; high-cost natural pesticides (quickly broken down by the elements) and the new technology of genetic weapons against insects can replace DDT and its deadly cousins; water eutrophication can be controlled by limiting fertilizer runoffs, phosphate-detergent use, and sewage-treatment-plant dumping. Some kinds of economic activity might be banned altogether—supersonic jet aircraft probably fit the category. But such limits hardly imply the end to growth.

Subtler forms of environmental damage caused by economic activity—weather change due to power generation is a prime candidate—are possibilities, but the best scientific evidence suggests that the probability of their reaching critical or irreversible levels in the next century has been exaggerated. One 1970 study, sponsored by MIT, weighs the merits of the doomsday scenarios and finds them wanting. Its report, based on the work of experts from a dozen disciplines ranging from meteorology to law, catalogues the possible global threats and finds none that constitutes a clear danger. But should we eventually identify specific threats to the global ecology, it is likely that solutions short of stopping the machinery of economic growth will be found. The most important lesson of ecology is caution; each step toward more sophisticated technology risks transgression against nature. But that same expansion of technology gives us the ability, if not the will, to recognize and avoid the hazards.

Affluence and Effluents

Economic growth, then, may or may not speed us on the path to doomsday, but it has certainly littered up the road. Urban sprawl, sulfur dioxide, dead fish, endangered species—all these are legitimately laid at the doorstep of the last few decades' economic expansion. And countless environmentalists not prone to predictions of apocalypse have concluded that every gain in prosperity takes its invariable toll in pollution. Survival may not be threatened by growth but human comfort is.

But this is an extrapolation of recent history, not a natural law. Pollution is not logically inherent in economic growth, nor has the linkage always been so immediate as it has lately appeared. Consider the *ambiance* of the eighteenth- or nineteenth-century city—blanketed by soot, layered with the excrement of horses and never far from that of men—and it becomes apparent that *some* kinds of pollution have diminished with affluence. If, in many cities, we have merely gotten the problem out of the chamberpots and into the waterways, that nonetheless might pass for progress.

To be sure, no such facile excuse can mitigate the

post-World War II pollution boom. Barry Commoner has argued that crucial industries—chemicals, fuels, fibers— have adopted new technologies whose effluent is more voluminous and more toxic than anything which went before. Conservationists less careful than Commoner have generalized this experience into a simple law: as Garrett Hardin puts it, Pollution = Population x Prosperity.

But the very fact that the postwar economy produced new pollutants through the application of novel technology suggests that Hardin's law is far from exact. Commoner says that most forms of pollution have increased from two to twenty times from 1946 to 1966, far exceeding the rate of economic advance. Economic growth does not carry with it a proportional increase in sludge. The increase may be far greater than proportional—as it has been—or considerably less, as it could be if we take corrective measures.

Pollution comes not simply from prosperity, but also from a system of incentives that encourage dirt-producing technologies. Change the incentives, and you can do something about pollution. In essence that is the economists' rebuttal to the zero-growth argument. Our basic environmental sin is not that we consume too many things, but that we produce them in the wrong way. Air and water have been free goods for manufacturers—nobody has made them pay for turning the biosphere into a giant garbage can. Naturally, industry took advantage of the privilege.

"The Name of the Game: Profit-Ability" was the 1970 slogan for Union Camp, a company whose paper-bag plant helps make the Savannah River one of the foulest sewers in the nation. The executive vice-president of the company, answering a Nader's Raiders charge that his firm was dangerously depleting groundwater supplies, replied, "I had my lawyers in Virginia research that, and they told us that we could suck the state of Virginia out through a hole in the ground, and there was nothing anyone could do about it." Union Camp's director of air and water protection noted for the benefit of *The New York Times* that "it probably won't hurt mankind a whole hell of a lot in the long run if the whooping crane doesn't quite make it."

Union Camp's executives may have been unusual in their public-be-fouled magniloquence, but surely not in their basic motivation. As Governor George Wallace remarked, apropos a Union Camp paper mill whose smoke reached twenty miles to Montgomery, "Yeah, that's the smell of money. She does smell sweet, don't it." Money talks, as well as deodorizes, and it has persuaded legislatures to slant the law in favor of polluters and against whooping cranes, asthma sufferers, and just plain people. And since polluters don't have to pay for the damage they do, they keep on polluting.

The profit motive for pollution, present throughout our history, seems recently to have intensified. As Commoner observes, "The new, more polluting technologies [seem to] yield higher profits than the older, less polluting technologies they have displaced." In some industries the connection between gain and garbage is especially perverse:

The extraordinarily high rate of profit of [the chemical] industry appears to be the direct result of the production at rapid intervals of new, usually unnatural, synthetic materials— which, entering the environment . . . often pollute it. This situation is an ecologist's nightmare, for in the four- or five-year period in which a new synthetic substance, such as a detergent or pesticide, is massively moved into the market—and into the environment—there is literally not enough time to work out its ecological effects. Inevitably, by the time the effects are known, the damage is done and the inertia of the heavy investment in new productive technology makes a retreat extraordinarily difficult.

"The very system of enhancing profit in this industry," concludes Commoner, "is precisely the cause of its intense, detrimental impact on the environment."

The task, then, is to break the bond between profits and pollution. Strategies far short of zero growth will do the job. Strict, detailed government regulations can simply order polluters to sweep up their wastes, profits notwithstanding. New taxes on discharges can force firms to pay the social cost of the damage they do—the price of producing the Sunday *New York Times,* for example, would include a charge for cleaning up after the mill that makes its newsprint, and another fee for carting away the paper on Monday morning. Government subsidies for pollution abatement could persuade firms to do research that they would otherwise find unprofitable.

The question for society is not an either/or choice about affluence vs. cleanliness, but a particularized choice about these less dramatic alternatives. Which method of control is most likely to survive political hazards? Which reduces pollution at the least cost in human labor and materials? Which minimizes the dislocation caused by abandoning our pro-dumping set of rules?

So far, these have not been the questions most environmentalists have asked (Commoner being a rare and outstanding exception). Their most publicized strategy is self-denial.

If you told the suburbanite that the way his house was built, the elimination of food-producing land that it caused, his long-distance drive to work, his work in the military-industrial-governmental structure, his use of power gadgets, his wife's consumption of clothing, his family's consumption of prepackaged synthetic goods, the daily pouring of thousands of food calories into the "garbage" disposal under his kitchen sink, and the birth of his third child are making the world unlivable, he wouldn't believe you.

Get him to believe you.

So advises *The Environmental Handbook,* the official program guide for 1970 Earth Day. Dirck Van Sickle's handbook on "Good Earth-keeping in America" adds some practical advice: "Nylon stockings or panty hose can be rolled into loose, airy balls and used as quilt stuffing." "If you go to market by car, don't use all that polluting horsepower just to haul yourself—take a friend. Don't shop together, however; going through the aisles encourages impulse buying." "Buy 'day-old' bread at the bakery, freeze and thaw it—it will taste fresh." Abstinence, once seen as the answer to the baby glut, has now been generalized to the entire spectrum of bodily pleasures and minor self-indulgences. Instead of throwing out that Coke bottle we are urged to tote it to the community recycling center; instead of eating what we please—or what we think healthy—we are told to mind each loaf's effect on the biosphere.

Eco-scrupulosity is good propaganda. If five thousand Palo Alto shoppers worry enough about the environment to change their buying habits, sooner or later their County Board of Supervisors may get the lesson. But as a strategy for directly curbing pollution, it has obvious limitations. Concerted self-inconveniencing by tens of millions of consumers would be necessary to make even a marginal impact on pollution. Air pollution in this country will be solved when the government gets the gumption to enforce some tough laws, not when every shopper makes sure to take along a friend.

In addition to encouraging consumer self-restraint, the aim of much ecological propaganda is of course to change the consciousness of businessmen. To a degree, this aim has been achieved. Not even an automobile executive would today echo the chutzpa of the classic 1953 letter from Ford to a Los Angeles County supervisor, quoted by Nader's air-pollution team: "The Ford engineering staff, although mindful that automobile engines produce gases, feels that these waste vapors are dissipated in the atmosphere quickly and do not present an air-pollution problem. Therefore our research department has not conducted any experimental work aimed at totally eliminating these gases." What the auto companies have done since then (at least, according to a Justice Department civil antitrust suit that the Nixon Administration conveniently settled out of court) was to agree among themselves mutually to delay the introduction of pollution-control equipment. And, apart from any alleged private conspiracies, the Big Three have been quite amiable in their public common front against the new, stiff antipollution requirements of federal law. Meanwhile, they, like the oil companies, paper manufacturers, and other new-found friends of the environment, have been furiously advertising their conversion to earth-worship. One is tempted to color them green.

What all this amounts to is open to question. No doubt businesses pollute less now that the public considers it immoral than they did when governors rhapsodized about smoke's smell of money. But this margin of difference isn't what will save the dying ocelot or enhance the average life span. Real social progress in this country—on those occasions when it has not simply come from economic growth—has required legislation. Pollution is a federal case.

Saying that, however, does not resolve the matter. There are better and worse ways to legislate the cleanup—a choice which involves how fast the work will go, how much it will cost, and who will pay the bill. These matters deserve mention.

An appealing, simple answer is to ban pollution altogether. A Nader water-pollution report calls for "instituting a 'no dumping' policy everywhere." The Senate passed, 86 to 0, a bill for a "national goal" of zero discharge of industrial wastes by 1985. That remedy is certainly tidy. But it is also grossly and pointlessly expensive. Removing 100 per cent of industrial discharges is estimated to be three times as costly as 97-per-cent removal—and often serves no real purpose. Streams have a natural capacity to assimilate limited amounts of certain waste; the fact that we have been scandalously abusing that capacity is no argument for ignoring it altogether. Moreover, even if industrial discharges were halted completely, runoffs of fertilizer (both chemical and natural) and sewage spillover from city storm drains would continue to pollute rivers. These too could be reduced, but by nothing approaching the 100-per-cent target for industrial wastes. As the Harvard economist Marc Roberts has argued, "The only shortcomings [of the no-dumping proposal] are that it is impossible, and if it were possible, it would be preposterously wasteful."

Whatever we do, some waterways some of the time will not be pure enough to wash a surgeon's hands. But there is no reason why they should be. For both health and recreational reasons, we need rivers and lakes that are vastly purer than at present. But at some point, as Roberts says, "even the fish won't notice the difference." There is no reason to make cleanliness an absolute value, taking precedence over all other ways of using the $316 billion needed for the job. Turning every drop of flowing water into an example for the world is no more sensible a goal for the 1970s than putting a shopping center on the moon would have been for the 1960s. It is, unfortunately, even more a temptation of the times.

A related if less extreme strategy is at the core of proposals favored by both Congressional Republicans and Democrats. The notion is to require every pollution source to make an across-the-board percentage cut in emissions. To reduce over-all pollution by 85 per cent, you require each plant to cut its own contribution by 85 per cent—regardless of where the plant is located or how much the abatement would cost. Again, the strategy seems straightforward, but it is administratively complicated and needlessly expensive. Different plants and industries have widely varying costs for pollution control. Some could eliminate close to 100 per cent of their pollutants at minimal cost; for others, even a modest cleanup is hugely expensive. A far more efficient way to achieve the desired reduction in total pollution would be to cut back emissions at those plants where the cutting is easiest. The cost differences between the two approaches—proportional reductions and "least cost" cutbacks—are substantial, on the order of 100 per cent. A 1969 study by Robert N. Grosse estimated that a "typical city" of 2 million persons, attempting to reduce human exposure to sulfur dioxides and particulates in smog would have to spend $1.26 billion using the proportional approach, compared with $769 million using a least-cost strategy. A Delaware estuary study showed "that a dissolved oxygen level of at least 3 parts per million [dis-

solved oxygen is a commonly used index of water quality]
would cost about twice as much with uniform treatment as a
least-cost solution."

A related problem is that the cost of pollution abatement
sharply increases as greater and greater abatement is
achieved. In beet-sugar plants, for example, a one-pound reduction in "biochemical oxygen demand" (b.o.d., a measure
of pollution) costs less than \$1 when only 30 per cent of the
b.o.d. has already been removed, but when 95 per cent has
been eliminated, the cost of removing an extra pound shoots
up to \$60. For water pollution in general, the Council of
Economic Advisers has estimated that it would cost \$60 bil-
lion to remove 87 per cent of the effluent; \$58 billion extra
for an additional 10 per cent; and \$200 billion on top of that
for the remaining three percentage points.

The lesson is not to make do with the pollution we have,
but to pay some attention to costs in choosing a strategy of
abatement and in deciding which pollutants must be nearly
completely eliminated and for which there are more modest,
acceptable targets. In the case of health hazards, such as sulfur oxides and particulates, something very close to 100-per-
cent elimination in populated areas makes good sense. But
other forms of pollution involve inconvenience, not death or
disaster. Saying that there is no acceptable level of pollution
is like saying that there is no acceptable level of auto
accidents—a fine proposition, though not one commensurate
with a reasonable expenditure of what, even in our affluent
society, are limited resources. The fact that both pollution
and auto accidents can be drastically reduced at modest cost
(and long ago should have been) is no argument for pretending to aim at an absolutely perfect record. We won't make it
—and, in the process of trying, we are more likely simply to

substitute the unlimited dumping of money for the unlimited dumping of wastes.

The record of federal water-pollution programs offers blunt confirmation of this danger. In 1956, Congress authorized federal grants to states for construction of municipal waste-treatment facilities. After thirteen years and $1.272 billion of federal donations, the General Accounting Office found that the program had "no appreciable effect on reducing pollution, improving water quality or enhancing the use of the waterways." Municipal treatment plants, where they existed, would clean up industrial wastes for free. So businesses kept on polluting, since it didn't cost them anything. Their volume of dreck exceeded anything the municipal plants could take out.

Another form of federal subsidy, tax incentives for firms to buy pollution-control equipment, was enthusiastically adopted by Congress in 1969. But this kind of tax "kicker" warps the firm's choice of methods for reducing waste. In many industries, it would be cheaper to alter the basic processes or technology to produce less effluent in the first place, rather than buy new equipment to clean it up. But the tax law merely encourages firms to generate muck and then make it pure—a precise contemporary equivalent of digging holes and filling them up again.

Through wasteful treatment-plant subsidies and casual tax giveaways, the Treasury rather than the biosphere has been taking a trip to the cleaners. All this might be forgiven if the burden fell on those who reap the greatest benefits from clean water, and who can afford to pay for government and private antipollution efforts. But for the most part it is the rich who go sailing while the poor pay sales taxes. As Marc Roberts writes:

Studies of outdoor recreation repeatedly show higher percentage of use by those in higher income groups. Indeed the streams and rivers that flow through downtown areas, and are accessible to the urban poor by public transportation, will often be the last waterways to be cleaned up—if they are ever made usable. Such rivers are usually the most polluted by industrial output, shipping, commercial and domestic wastes and the storm runoffs from urban streets.

Little is said about income distribution in the usual conservationist argument—it seems to be a touchy subject. Even the otherwise thorough 1971 Report of the President's Council on Environmental Quality barely grazes the question. The poor, the Council notes, have much to gain from cleaner air. Nothing is said about what the poor gain from pristine lakes which they cannot afford to visit, or how much they lose from higher regressive taxes and product prices. It is probably too optimistic to expect society's decision for cleaner surroundings to be accompanied by income redistribution—or improved access—for the urban poor. But one can at least demand a decent watch on costs since they will fall so heavily on those who least deserve them.

To economists, the core of an efficient solution must be a shift in business incentives. The answer, they argue, is not to stop production, but to charge for pollution. For many kinds of pollution, the technology of abatement is already well developed—all that's needed is a change in incentives. Jackhammer compressor noise, for example, could be reduced 99 per cent by the use of a quiet compressor, which adds only about 10 or 15 per cent to cost. But today builders have no reason to shell out their money to protect other people's ears. A "noise tax" could change their minds. The price of a livable environment by this reasoning is not an end to growth, but an end to freeloading. If firms paid their annual cleanup costs in the form of a tax, it would amount to less than 1.5 per cent of GNP. The price is not small—$18 billion a year by 1975, assuming that the job is done efficiently —but it puts much of the stop-growth-or-die rhetoric in its place. We can, say the economists, afford to eat our cake and pick up the wrapper, too.

A couple of reservations must be added to the argument for pollution taxes. Taxes on water pollution give industries the right incentive to choose less effluent-prone technologies, but they encourage firm-by-firm efforts at water purification. Often, it would be far more economical to treat wastes at a common plant, taking advantage of substantial economies of scale. For this reason, Roberts and others have proposed the creation of regional river-basin authorities. Authorities would be told to clean up their rivers and pay for it with a service charge on polluters. Since businesses would have to pay a fee for dumping, they would dump a lot less. Their fees would be used to clean up the remainder, as efficiently as possible.

The electric-power crisis illustrates the uses and limitations of pollution taxes. Today, there is a direct conflict between clean air and electric power. Con Ed's coal- and oil-burning power stations generate 40 per cent of the chemical pollutants and 10 per cent of the smoke in New York City. Proposed expansion of the region's power capacity would be made at additional cost to the environment—more fossil-fuel facilities increase air pollution, while nuclear plants create thermal pollution and raise unresolved issues of safety. Recognizing the dangers, environmental groups have rallied to block further construction. The result—annual summer power shortages with no relief in sight.

Economists claim that the dilemma is artificial; the root of the problem is the gap between the price consumers pay for electricity and its actual social cost. As Redi-Kilowatt used to inform us, "Electricity is the biggest bargain in your family budget"; but the monthly power bill never included the cost to emphysema sufferers in Queens.

The gap between price and cost reduces the incentives for consumers to make reasonable economies in daily use—if rates were, say, double what they are now, many of us *would* shut off the lights and turn down the air conditioner. Bargain rates also encourage the choice of electricity over more ecologically benign sources of power. Home heating and commercial air-conditioning electricity rates are good examples. Large users are actually charged less per kilowatt hour. Yet the use of electric heating and cooling at least doubles the amount of sulfur-dioxide emissions. Taxes on air polluters, like taxes on water polluters, would both cut pollution levels and pass on the costs of defiling the environment to those who benefit.

Pollution taxes not only would help to clean up the air by reducing the demand for electricity, but would provide direct incentives to the power companies to reduce effluents. Until recently, nobody was much interested in designing methods to cut smokestack sulfur emissions or remove sulfur from fuels before they were burned. The power industry was unwilling to pay more for cleaner air because no one insisted. But now, with public pressure creating that insistence, the Nixon Administration has proposed a sulfur-dioxide emission charge and a tax on leaded gasoline. However, again, taxes alone may not be sufficient to motivate business to use the cheapest antipollution technology. Promising new approaches to abatement in more speculative areas may languish for lack of research funds. For example, it may be feasible to convert fossil fuels directly into electricity without the intermediate step of generating steam to run turbines. The net result could be a dramatic reduction in the amount of damage that each kilowatt does to the environment. One direct-conversion method, the fuel cell, has already provided utility power for manned space flights. But we will not know if large-scale power plants are practical until someone spends the money to find out. Federal subsidies are probably a prerequisite for progress.

Another tack is to move power facilities away from the cities. Electricity could be produced in huge generating stations at isolated sites and transported thousands of miles to where it's used. The idea is not new: the Soviet Union has committed vast resources to long-distance, high-tension power transmission, because they believe it is cheaper. While this approach does not reduce pollution, it would confine its worst effects to places where few people live.

In sum, there is not a stark choice between escalating filth or a stagnating economy. Modest expenditures on pollution control can yield enormous improvements. (London, for example, has cut smoke emissions by 80 per cent over the past fifteen years; since the introduction of well-planned sewage treatment, fish have reappeared in the Thames. The cost of the cleanup of London air has been about 36 cents per year for each Greater London resident.) If the task of cleaning up is organized efficiently, the costs of high standards of air and water quality will be bearable—certainly less than one-tenth of GNP, the amount added by two good years of growth.

Hence, stopping growth would be a sane way to protect the environment only if society does not have the nerve to do the job directly. But a world too timid to require smokestack precipitators would hardly jump at the chance to shut down factories. Conversely, if we ever did have the will power to halt growth, we could use that resolve affirmatively to enhance the quality of life and eliminate any threat to its continuation.

Growth and Imperialism

Despoiling the environment is but one of the recent charges against growth. Robbing other countries of their natural riches is another. "The internal prosperity of the United States," wrote Claude Julien in *America's Empire,* "depends in very large part on its freedom of access to the natural resources of the entire world and more especially of the poor countries"—hence the presence of American corporations abroad and the motive for American militarism. In the wake of countless American military adventures this view has attracted converts across the political spectrum: Julien is the foreign editor of France's centrist daily, *Le Monde.*

The argument is a venerable one. Lenin wrote in 1920 that capitalism has created "a handful . . . of exceptionally rich and powerful states which plunder the whole world simply by 'clipping coupons.' " Imperialism was "the highest stage of capitalism," a necessary culmination of the search not merely for raw materials but for markets to sop up the surplus production of domestic industry. Economic growth of the rich capitalist states, according to this thesis, requires control and immiserization of the poor.

Each step of the argument demands attention. Would the American economy stop dead in its tracks if it could no longer tank up on foreign fuel? Do our commodity purchases from Third World nations exploit their citizens and subjugate their governments? Do we depend on them, do they suffer because of us, or both?

The first question is the easiest. America's ties to the world economy have always been modest in this century. And these ties are probably loosening. The United States imports only about 5 per cent of her national income (in contrast to almost 20 per cent for Britain and 10 per cent for Japan). One good year's growth—say, the $63-billion gain in real GNP from 1965 to 1966—exceeds the total American import bill. Current import levels for these products could be reduced with only minor irritation as most United States imports are not scarce raw materials, but compete directly with products made at home. At worst, Toyota buyers would have to settle for Pintos, and California Burgundies would take the place of the real thing. Most important raw materials, too, are in domestic supply: if the United States were to stop trading with Chile and Zambia, the telephone company could still get copper wire, though it might have to pay twice the price. America's huge geographical scope and her diverse productive structure make her economy virtually self-sufficient.

There are, to be sure, some few materials presently essential for industrial production that simply must be obtained abroad. It takes chromium to make specialized steel products, and most of the world's chromium is in the Soviet Union and Africa. Another vital metal, manganese, must be imported from India, Africa, or Latin America. So it is fair to say that, under current technology, the American industrial system does marginally depend on the availability of these crucial minerals. But this dependence does not hinge on growth. Even if the American economy grew no further, a cessation of all imports of chromium and a depletion of all stockpiles would for a while cripple the steel industry. Conversely, rapid economic growth would not necessarily increase this vulnerability. In the short run we might feel the pinch even more severely, but, as we suggested earlier, growth creates the technological resources to free us from raw-material dependency. A growing economy with an enormous scientific and engineering establishment can, with far greater ease than a stagnant one, accommodate an increase in recycling, or develop an alternative to scarce minerals. Spectacular innovations made under the pressure of wartime necessity, such as the development of synthetic ammonia and artificial rubber, have been matched over the past decades by hundreds of new processes that free the economy from dependence on foreign resources. Of course, imports continue to be used since they are often cheaper. But, should the need arise, the American economy could make the adjustment to virtual self-sufficiency with little loss to the consumer in the long run.

A common corollary to the need-for-raw-materials thesis is what Julien calls the "vital need . . . to export manufactured goods." But, similarly, exports play a modest role in American business, representing only a tiny fraction of total output. Chicago is a better market for computers than all of Southeast Asia. Ford and General Motors' profits on domestic sales alone probably exceed the total profit made by all American corporations on their export sales.

Exports, according to the imperialism thesis, mean jobs for American workers, and a curtailment of foreign sales would aggravate unemployment and accelerate the capitalist crisis. As with many of these arguments, there exists a Nixon as well as a Lenin version of the liturgy. The Nixon Administration's demands for reduced Japanese and European trade barriers, and for an export-promoting devaluation of the dollar, were sold domestically by harping on the new jobs in store for American workers.

Here again, the real effect is negligible. If exports were halted, the resulting slack in American industry could be taken up by new domestic demand. Expansionary fiscal and monetary policy could buoy the home economy and fully compensate for the jobs lost in export production. If the Japanese won't buy our tractor-trailers, and the Europeans turn their backs on Maryland chickens, we are not condemned to an escalating recession. A tax cut for American consumers or an increase in government spending would keep production humming and fill the employment gap.

To be sure, American governments do not customarily pursue a full-employment policy. During the Depression, exports were important for jobs because FDR still believed in a balanced budget; in a pre-Keynesian world, the necessary domestic measures would not be taken to compensate for diminished foreign demand. And even since Keynes, expansion has usually been stopped short of the point of full employment. But the main reason for the curb on employment is a fear of inflation linked to high-capacity production. That inflation, in turn, exists whether the source of demand for American products is foreign or domestic. A Japanese housewife's yen for American soybeans creates the same pressure on American prices as demand from the Illinois manufacturer of synthetic bacon chips. Thus a reduction in exports would allow American policy-makers to generate an equivalent increase in domestic demand without aggravating the pressure on prices. If our work force remains underemployed, it is not because of the disappearance of overseas markets but rather of our continuing unwillingness to risk a higher rate of inflation.

Likewise, there is little to the argument that U.S. corporations need foreign subsidiaries to mop up their surplus capital. Domestic investment in plant and equipment overshadows the highly visible expansion of American corporate subsidiaries abroad. For every dollar invested in foreign enterprises since World War II, at least fifteen have been invested at home. Business made a $5-billion profit on direct foreign investments in 1968 but earned $89 billion in the United States that same year. It is true that the profit rate on foreign investment has averaged higher than the return on domestic projects. But, however attractive these "superprofits" (Lenin's term) are to U.S. corporations or business-minded Presidents, they are in no sense *necessary* to the health and welfare of American capitalists. If all U.S. properties abroad were suddenly confiscated, individual shareholders would be gored but the total wealth of America's rich would be diminished by at most only a few per cent.

Nonetheless, economic gain cannot be dismissed as a motive of American foreign-policy-makers simply because the nation's well-being is not at stake. The interests of the privileged often take precedence—in both international and domestic politics. Congress did not donate hundreds of millions to the Lockheed Corporation because the United States needed another aircraft manufacturer, nor is the farm-subsidy program maintained for the general welfare. And we certainly don't need a Weatherman to tell us that foreign policy toward Latin America and the Middle East has long been practiced for (and by) American business. As United States Marine Corps General Smedley D. Butler bragged in days long before Richard Nixon: "I helped make

Mexico safe for American oil interests in 1914. I helped make Haiti and Cuba a decent place for the National City Bank boys to collect revenue in. . . . I helped make Honduras 'right' for American fruit companies."

American corporations with investments abroad exercise a disproportionate influence in domestic politics. Raymond Vernon surveyed the *Fortune* 500—the 500 largest U.S. industrial corporations, measured by sales—and found only 187 with manufacturing subsidiaries in six or more countries. But these 187 enterprises, he observed, "prove to be an extraordinary group, quite distinct in many respects from the rest of the U.S. corporate economy." They accounted in 1966 for $209 billion in sales, or approximately 39 per cent of the total sales of all U.S. manufacturing enterprises. Compared with their brethren in the *Fortune* 500, they were several times as large, more heavily involved in advertising, research, and development, and somewhat more profitable. It requires no fevered revolutionary imagination—only a look at Jack Anderson's columns—to see in these corporations, and in the banks and financial institutions which interconnect them, the directorate of American capitalism.

On the other hand, the forces that move American foreign policy are more complicated than simple subservience to the interests of giant cosmopolitan corporations. The Vietnam War was not really about America's lust-for-oil concessions in the Mekong delta, any more than the Korean War reflected our anticipation of profitable investment south of the 38th parallel. Today, two decades after the Korean truce, South Korea is a bustling capitalist economy and some American corporations migrate there to produce transistor radios. But other American companies, stuck with domestic plants that must compete with cheap imports, would just as soon see

Korea disappear, if not into communism at least into seraphic backwardness.

The driving force behind the Cold War has not been country-by-country concerns about investment opportunities or raw materials. We burned more oil in bombing raids than we are ever likely to pump out of Vietnam. But these economic concerns have played a part in the over-all geopolitical rationalizations for U.S. foreign policy. Ask a mid-1960s hawk why Vietnam was so important for American security, and he would probably say something about the domino theory and the fall of Indonesia. Indonesia, in turn, was vital because her rich oil and mineral reserves could not be allowed to fall into Communist hands. The Japanese believed in a Greater South-East Asia Co-Prosperity Sphere, and so did we.

But lust for raw materials is no more than a partial explanation for America's global strategy. The United States has fretted about Southeast Asia not so much because it is rich as because it is there. Communist victories in Asia would mean more red splotches on the Situation Room map. Far more than any mundane concerns about Indonesian oil or Malaysian tin, this vision of ideological combat and threatened encirclement has sent America to war.

In sum, America's perceived need for foreign raw materials has only modest significance for American foreign policy. Slow or zero economic growth in the United States would weaken the objective argument for American interventionism —but this argument was shaky to begin with, and never really formed the basis for policy. Conceivably, a zero-growth strategy might reflect a certain contentment with our lot, which might save us from foreign adventures as well as domestic striving. But it seems equally likely that a stagnant economy would simply aggravate our irritability in foreign affairs.

While foreign trade and investment have little impact on the American economy, the same cannot be said of the United States' commercial partners. For some underdeveloped countries, like Saudi Arabia and Liberia, the American presence completely dominates economic activity. For most others, American markets are vital simply because what America imports from them represents a substantial portion of their total exports.

What happens to impoverished nations whose export economies are linked to the U.S. market? To many observers, the pattern is predictable—and not very pretty. The foreign investor sets up a self-contained enclave within the host country. With its own highly paid technicians, its company stores for local workers, and fenced-off housing for foreign personnel, it amounts to a self-governing principality of American masters and local serfs. Instead of using local processing facilities and encouraging the development of domestic industry, the foreign company simply scoops up minerals and sends them home for transformation. Initially, at least, it pays little or no royalties to the foreign government but, rather, a small contribution in graft. Later, renegotiated contracts may substantially change the split of the take. The winners are not the local masses, but tawdry elites whose fancy airports and chauffeured Mercedeses are financed with export earnings. If exports do promote any domestic growth, it is of the most lopsided and vulnerable kind. Every mountain and hill is made low, but the valleys are not exalted. Cities built on oil or copper wealth teem with millions of transplanted peasants. Rural poverty is transformed into urban squalor. If the export boom should ever collapse—a virtually inevitable cycle, say the critics—the country will be left with its bloated population and malignant cities, depleted mines and empty coffers.

It is not hard to find cases which snugly fit the pattern. Jonathan Levin has chronicled the case of nineteenth-century Peru and its guano boom—a fittingly pungent tale of foreign greed (in this case, largely British) and domestic misfortune. In the 1830s, visiting foreign merchants smelled money in the desert islands off the coast of Peru, whose mountain-high bird droppings, untouched by rain, were rich in plant-nurturing nitrogen. In 1840, the Peruvian government gave a six-year contract to a local entrepreneur and his Liverpool financier. The first load of guano, forwarded to Britain on the good ship *Bonanza,* fetched a pretty price on the London fertilizer market. Soon the business was booming, and additional foreign and Peruvian capitalists got out their shovels. Agitation developed to take the treasure out of foreign hands, and some influential Limeño businessmen ousted the British contractors. But world demand for guano outstripped their limited ability to raise capital, attract labor, and develop channels for marketing. Within two decades, the foreigners were back—this time with a fat royalty to the government. Miscellaneous guano sidelines created a thriving native entrepreneurial class. Nicolás de Piérola, a twenty-three-year-old Peruvian divinity student and newspaper editor, dropped his columns of theological disputation and began the first guano trade journal. Later the young man became President.

For labor, the guano companies imported thousands of Chinese coolies under eight-year transferable indentures. Conditions were so atrocious—desert temperatures and unremitting labor—that constant patrol was necessary to keep the Chinese workers from flinging themselves off the guano cliffs and into the enfolding sea.

While the boom continued, the government used its royalty revenues to replace taxes—including the hated head tax on the indigenous Indian population. Soon the revenues exceeded even this goal and cried out for new uses. New uses were found. The guano-rich Peruvian entrepreneurial class proposed a scheme for economic development: the building of modern railroads, from nowhere to nowhere. Bonds, floated on the European market, were backed by guano revenues for decades to come. Peruvian contractors got rich, and gleaming railway tracks adorned the desert.

But then the guano ran out. After forty years of exploitation and over $6 billion in retail sales, the guano boom was over. The Peruvian government was left with some useless railways, a fattened upper middle class, and an enormous foreign debt. By 1876 the debt was in default, foreign credit became unavailable, and Peru plunged into a disastrous war over nitrate lands.

At least the first part of this history—initial foreign involvement, parasitic intervention by wealthy domestic interests, rising payments to the government siphoned off for worthless prestige projects—has dozens of recent counterparts. Increasing investment in Liberia by the Firestone Tire and Rubber Company made Africa's first black independent nation of modern times into a virtual subsidiary of an American corporation. Under a 1926 agreement, in return for a $2.25-million, 7-per-cent loan, the Liberian government agreed to subject all its financial decisions to the approval of an "adviser," nominated by the President of the United States on the suggestion of the Firestone board of directors. In 1952 the loan was paid off, and the Tubman Administration in Liberia erected a monument to President Tubman, "dedicated to the great relief brought to the country by the Tubman Administration in the retirement of the 1926 loan with its humiliating and strangulating effects. . . ." But to this day, the national currency of Liberia remains the U.S. dollar—making Liberia about as capable of running an independent economic policy as Des Moines. Liberian law provides that the forms and regulations of the Liberian Army shall be those of the U.S. Army, unless otherwise specified. One is tempted to imagine the issuance of stock certificates in place of passports, and lopsided proxy counts performing the office of lopsided elections.

But even in these stark examples of corporate imperialism, one finds some possible credit entries on the balance sheet. A small fraction of Peru's guano gains did trickle down to the Indian population, now freed from the head tax. Firestone did build some schools and houses for its Liberian employees, though of course it found integrated facilities "impracticable." Well before Firestone hired Liberian tribesmen as tree tappers and installed its advisers in the Monrovia customs house, the tribes were subject to the relentless exploitation of the Liberian-American ruling class, descendants of the freed American slaves who founded the nation in 1830.

Is trickle-down development better than no development at all? Is cruel and exploitative modernization an advance over aboriginal poverty? Was development under a Socialist or an honest nationalist regime a realistic alternative to foreign exploitation? These are complicated questions of fact, values, and pure speculation. In some countries where nationalist development might have been possible, foreign investment has served to entrench a reactionary local ruling class. South Africa buys modern jet aircraft and antiriot tanks with the royalties from diamond and gold mines. Guatemala's social revolution was suppressed by CIA agents defending our banana interests. In other cases a more dialectical process has been at work: economic development itself has set in motion the forces for revolution or nonrevolutionary social change. Foreign enclaves have created new sources of wealth and power which competed with the quasi-feudal economic base of traditional elites. Resentment of foreign exploitation has itself been the stimulus for domestic upheaval.

None of this is meant to argue that unrestricted American investment has been, or will be, a good thing for the world's poor. Vastly more humane alternatives for social change are easy to conceive and, in many cases, might have been likely in the absence of Yankee expansion. But, again, we are convinced that halting American economic growth is a blunt and ineffective formula for detoxifying our influence on the world. The 1954 recession did not inhibit American intervention in Guatemala, nor did the 1958 recession stay our hand in Lebanon. Weak business conditions at home may simply promote more aggressive corporate self-seeking abroad. We see no reason to sacrifice the future of America's poor for the uncertain promise of a better future for the world's poor.

2

Sharing the Wealth:
Income Redistribution as
an Alternative to Growth

Two myths about the distribution of income comforted
many liberals during the 1950s. Incomes, they believed, were
becoming steadily more equal, and government spending
programs uniformly accelerated that trend. Frederick Lewis
Allen spoke for a self-satisfied New Deal generation when he
said, "we had brought about a virtually automatic redistribution of income from the well-to-do to the less well-to-do"
through the mechanism of the welfare state.

In fact, the distribution of income in the United States
has remained virtually immobile since the end of World
War II, and many of the liberals' most cherished public programs take money from the poor and give it to the upper
middle class. The government has not consistently played
Robin Hood; often it has acted more on the order of the
Sheriff of Nottingham.

If pressed, most liberals would now admit this. But their attitudes toward economic growth betray the continuing strength of the myth of egalitarian progress. Today's mood of disenchantment with growth reflects, in large part, the assumption that the problems of the poor may yet be solved by the redistributive measures of the welfare state or the progressive leveling of incomes through improved education. With redistribution left to do the heavy work of social reform, growth can be treated as a concern only of the affluent, and then dismissed.

Rarely is any of this reasoning made explicit, nor could it be. Since the late 1950s, no one familiar with the statistics could argue that America was on the path to economic equality. But the belief in social progress has been sturdy enough to survive the evidence of its frustration. It is a belief that has served historically important needs and cannot be casually abandoned.

A word on this background goes far to explain the current politics of growth. Postwar liberals were seeking to establish their title to the middle ground of American politics—equidistant from the Communist-tinged left and the conservative right. Arthur M. Schlesinger, Jr., called this turf "the vital center" and claimed it for the heirs of the New Deal, "the politicians, the administrators, the doers [as opposed to] the sentimentalists, the utopians, the wailers" of the left.

Central to this claim was a rhapsodic vision of social engineering ("For the doer," said Schlesinger, "the essential form of democratic education is the taking of great decisions under the burden of civic responsibility") and a generous view of its accomplishments ("The capitalist state," he proclaimed, "far from being the helpless instrument of the possessing classes has become the means by which other groups have redressed the balance of social power against the rich and the well-born"). When Schlesinger wrote these words, in 1949, the evidence was not yet in on the path of income distribution over the New Deal years. But by the early 1960s, liberals began to acknowledge the persistence of inequality in the private sector. New statistics showed that income distribution had barely changed since the war. In 1948, the poorest 20 per cent of the nation's families shared only 5 per cent of the nation's income; by 1955, they had to make do with 4.8 per cent. Between 1948 and 1955, the percentage of families earning less than one half the median income—a good measure of relative poverty—increased a little less than one percentage point.

Liberals reacted to these revelations by redoubling their faith in spending by the public sector. John Kenneth Galbraith's 1958 book, *The Affluent Society,* summed up the new strategy. Galbraith argued that inequality could not be attacked directly through a stiffer income tax. Most Americans, he observed, were too prosperous to care very much about soaking the rich. Thus equality had faded as a political issue. It could be approached only indirectly, through a general expansion of public spending. The poor, Galbraith argued, "would be among the first beneficiaries of [government spending on] education, health, housing and other services." Admittedly, an enlarged public sector would support itself in major part through regressive taxation, for example by hiking sales taxes. But that was no objection:

> It will be argued that some people are still very poor. The sales tax, unlike the income tax, weighs heavily on the small consumption of such individuals. But if the income tax is unavailable or in service to other ends, the only alternative is to sacrifice social balance [between public and private spending].

. . . The modern liberal rallies to protect the poor from the taxes which, in the next generation, as the result of higher investment in their children, would eliminate poverty.

Conversely, Galbraith argued, growth by itself would do little for the poor: "There is no assurance," he wrote in 1960, "merely from expanding output *per se* that the benefit will accrue to those at the bottom of the pyramid who need the goods the most."

Galbraith's ideology made virtuous what liberal politicians had already found necessary: a program that did not rely on the defunct Roosevelt coalition of labor and the ethnic minorities. The first hope of postwar liberals had been for a continuation of the New Deal, extending its range of social programs and maintaining its old adherents. The Labour government in Great Britain was consolidating the wartime mood of national unity into a broad coalition for the welfare state, and America's liberal Democrats thought, since years of "war socialism" had blurred ideological distinctions, they could do the same for the federal government.

The early results were encouraging. In 1945, a bipartisan group of congressmen, with Representative Everett Dirksen as co-chairman, began lobbying for federal aid to elementary and secondary education. Senator Robert Taft joined forces with the education lobby and led a drive for a massive national housing program. Congress voted to reorganize and expand public health programs in 1944, and in 1946 passed without significant opposition the Hill-Burton Act, inaugurating a five-year, $375-million program of federal assistance for hospital construction. The Employment Act of 1946 made it the "continuing policy and responsibility of the Federal Government, to promote maximum employment, production and purchasing power" and embodied the formal reception of Keynesianism into national policy.

The 1946 elections packed the Congress with conservatives, but President Truman fought and won the 1948 election on an aggressively liberal program, demanding action on housing, aid to education, health care, civil rights, public power, extensions of social security, and an increase in the minimum wage. In 1949, Congress was presented with a national health-insurance plan, labeled "creeping socialism" by the AMA; a comprehensive housing bill, labeled "creeping socialism" by the real-estate lobby; and a revamped agricultural program, labeled "creeping socialism" by the large farmers. The health bill would, indeed, have given every American health insurance under Social Security. The housing bill called for "the realization as soon as feasible of the goal of a decent home and suitable living environment for every American family" and proposed $1.5 billion for urban renewal and almost $500 million for low-cost public housing. The "Brannan Plan" for agriculture would have changed the federal farm program from one which gouged consumers and enriched large farmers to a plan of income support for small farmers and low product prices for the consumer. Never before or since (with the possible exception of the New Deal's one hundred days) has so vast a program of reform been seriously debated by Congress.

But what Truman achieved was a debate, not a victory. The health-insurance plan was killed by the multimillion-dollar opposition of the doctors' lobby; Southern cotton growers and large Midwestern farmers cut down the Brannan Plan; the housing bill passed, only to see its public-housing targets mocked year after year by stingy appropriations. The final Housing Act of 1949 called for construction of 135,000 units of low-income public housing each year for six years. But each year Congressional conservatives would restage the battle against public housing in the House Appropriations and Rules committees; the final appropriations bill would slash the number of housing starts below the 1949 target. In 1951, the appropriations ceiling was set at 50,000 units; in 1952, 35,000; in 1953, 20,000; the 1954 appropriations bill contained no funds for new housing starts and in the ten months after its passage precisely 142 units were begun. The New Deal was over.

While the liberal legislative program was falling apart in Congress, the Roosevelt electoral coalition was being dismembered at the polls. Many upwardly mobile voters from the white ethnic groups removed themselves from the New Deal alliance of underdogs. Farmers and white-collar workers—Roosevelt supporters, thanks to the Depression—were rediscovering their Republican past. Only blacks, deep Southerners, and militant union members could be counted on to stay put.

The lesson for liberals was that they could succeed only with new measures and new partners; over the life of the Eisenhower Administration these shifts were executed. Congressional Democrats revamped the traditional liberal public programs, invented new ones, and shifted priorities among old ones, to appeal to a middle-class electorate and a newly emerging business constituency.

The history of urban renewal typifies the process. Urban renewal was initially an Eisenhower program, renamed and expanded from the urban redevelopment program of the 1949 Housing Act. Federal funds were made available to tear down slums and replace them with new housing, stores, and industries. Communities were to develop comprehensive "workable programs" for eliminating blight, and millions of dollars were provided to nourish the new science of urban and regional planning. As urban renewal gained momentum, it won an increasingly enthusiastic Democratic constituency which made the program its own. Academic liberals were charmed by its unabashed commitment to "planning," previously a Republican hate-word, and by its utility as a backdoor route for publicly financed housing. Democratic mayors were delighted to use federal funds to banish slums from downtown business districts and build handsome middle-class apartment buildings and new stores for local merchants. Urban renewal, writes Leonard Chazen, outfitted mayors with a new image as "conciliatory figures above factional struggles for political power."

> In the mid-1950s, the "good" mayors began to be seen as high-minded representatives of "good government." It seemed that the time had passed when rascally mayors, like James Curley of Boston, discharged their obligations to the poor through extortion. The enlightened mayor cleaned up the city by replacing party hacks with blue-ribbon committees and downtown slums with high-risers. . . . The mayor's real task was to conciliate business as well as to satisfy the middle class's desire for a prosperous, well-ordered city. In return, the business community would enter into an alliance with the city social-service agencies and the Urban Renewal Authority to create "a better and more beautiful city for rich and poor alike."

None of this retained much appeal for Eisenhower, who by 1958 was yearning to turn the program over to the states and detach it from city-hall politics and the federal trough. By 1959, Eisenhower was ready to veto two housing bills, in part for their generosity toward urban renewal. The vetoes were sustained on a party-line vote, and urban renewal had become a Democratic program.

Federal grants for airports, a clear upper-income subsidy, also began with bipartisan support, but faced Eisenhower's veto in 1958. The President was "convinced that the time has come for the Federal government to begin an orderly withdrawal from the airport program" and that "aviation generally has achieved a state of maturity in which the users should be expected to pay an increasing share of airport costs." But Democrats on the House Interstate and Foreign Commerce Committee found the need for airport subsidies "almost self-evident" and passed a bill extending the program for two years until a new and presumably Democratic Administration "could legislate more wisely."

Farm policy was highly partisan throughout the Eisenhower years. Democrats, after the defeat of the Brannan Plan, supported high price supports for agricultural products which largely ended up in the pockets of prosperous farmers; Eisenhower and his scapegoat Secretary of Agriculture, Ezra Taft Benson, wanted lower prices and a restoration of market principles. Four times in his Administration Eisenhower vetoed major farm bills which would have propped up the high-price system. On the crucial votes, even big-city Democrats would often vote against low food prices; their motives ranged from pure partisanship, ideological sympathy with the small farmer, to an attempt to maintain a farmer-labor coalition which would help urban interests on social-welfare issues. In 1959 and 1960—when postwar liberals learned that even a heavily Democratic Congress would enact little progressive legislation—large groups of Northern Democrats deserted the farm bloc on price-support bills. But, in 1961, President Kennedy was able to muster their support for a high-price bill on a plea of party unity.

Some of the major public-sector programs of the 1950s retained bipartisan support. The grandest was the interstate-highway program, committing the federal government to a thirteen-year, $26-billion extension of asphalt. The highway plan passed Congress in 1956 by virtual acclamation, as did successive bills to meet the program's escalating cost. Briefly, in 1959, Democrats made an attempt to shift part of the financing of the highway program from highway-user taxes to general revenues obtained from closing loopholes in the income tax. In that year, almost half of the Democrats in the House voted against the $3.5-billion revenue increase. But, for highways as well as for agriculture, President Kennedy's election meant a renewed Democratic commitment to heavy spending. As the estimated federal cost for completing the interstate system rose from the initial $26 billion to $37 billion in 1961 and $50 billion in 1968, the Kennedy and Johnson Administrations automatically requested, and received, the needed extra revenues.

The burgeoning of the interstate-highway program did not spell the neglect of more traditional forms of pork. Democrats fought several pitched battles with the Eisenhower Administration over classic "rivers and harbors" programs. In 1959, for example, Eisenhower twice vetoed public-works bills that provided for dozens of new construction starts he had not requested. The vetoes produced remarkably straight party-line votes in a Congress normally split along ideological rather than partisan divisions; Democrats in the House, for example, voted 260 to 5 to override the veto, while amost six sevenths of the 136 Republicans voted to uphold it. Again, in 1963, a measure to add $450 million to the accelerated public-works program passed Congress on a partisan vote; only 30 Southern and 3 Northern Democrats joined the 151 Republicans opposing the plan. Liberal Democrats were drawn to the progam not simply because of its attractions to local constituencies, but as a means for fiscal stimulus to a weak economy. Lacking the votes for major housing, health, and education programs, they turned to the readiest available means for expanding the public sector.

While Congressional Democrats were courting middle-income voters with slum clearance, public works, and farm subsidies, liberals in state legislatures were turning their attentions to higher education. In the 1950s, state appropriations for college and university education more than doubled; in the 1960s, they increased an additional 337 per cent. California accelerated its spending for two-year colleges, planning eventually to offer some form of college education to all high-school graduates. In other states, liberals campaigned for similar extension of the state-university system to make, as one educator urged, "the American dream of equal opportunity finally come true."

The result of all this activity was a new, salable kit of programs for Democrats. But it was not a redistribution of income. Galbraith had assumed that a basically middle-class electorate could be hoodwinked into supporting a measure of equality through public spending that it would never endorse directly. If anything, the outcome was the reverse. The public programs of the 1950s built homes and roads for the middle classes, setting out on their epic migration from the central cities to surburbia. They provided college education for middle- and upper-middle-income groups so that not merely the sons and daughters of the rich, but also those of the merely affluent, could walk through ivy-covered halls. For the few per cent of the population which made heavy use of the airlines, the Democrats provided subsidized airports; for the one-tenth of one per cent who owned private airplanes, an even more generous ticket was written. The poor, for their part, were placed at the wrong end of a bulldozer.

Only in the mid-1960s, with the proclamation of the War on Poverty, did the federal government even attempt any new measures of income redistribution. But the total effect of Lyndon Johnson's program on the income share of the poor is barely visible. The contribution made by the Office of Economic Opportunity to the elimination of inequality in America is measurable in roughly the same terms as the Peace Corps' contribution to peace: possibly some real change in tone, vast amounts of ballyhoo, a useful training of cadres, and nothing one would care to measure in dollars or lives.

While the War on Poverty was raging, older programs for equality were in steady retreat. The income tax, long thought to be "progressive" in the technical sense—that is, imposing larger proportional burdens on higher incomes— was only minutely so during the 1950s, and during the 1960s even this progressivity was largely eroded. Rates were cut by the Kennedy Administration as part of its progrowth program, and new loopholes were added by Congress faster than the old ones plugged. Kennedy's investment-tax credit— designed to aid growth—incidentally reduced corporate taxes by $3 billion a year. The Medicare program, proposed under Kennedy and enacted under Johnson, was financed by increasing the strongly regressive Social Security tax. The liberal administrations of the 1960s took the Galbraith view of taxation—public programs were so desirable in themselves that you raised the money any way you could.

Sharing the Wealth 71

Recent years have brought vastly improved statistical studies on the question of income distribution and government programs. They confirm the durability of inequality in the private economy and the primarily passive role of the public sector, except for compulsory primary and secondary education, Social Security, and subsistence welfare for the very poor. The government provides other services to people in roughly the proportion that they pay taxes. The distribution of income among classes was even less mobile from 1957 to 1968 than in the previous decade. There was a shift along racial lines—the relative income of nonwhites increased from 51 per cent of the white median in 1958 to 63 per cent in 1968. But much of this change was due to black migration from the low-wage South and from rural to urban areas, not to waning discrimination or better education.

Taxes have only a small effect on the relative distribution of income. The progressive rates of the income tax are offset not merely by the well-known loopholes—capital gains, oil-depletion allowances—but by special deductions whose worthy purposes insulate them from political attack: e.g., deductions for mortgage payments, property taxes, charitable contributions, and extraordinary medical costs, or the exemption for Social Security earnings. Each of these provisions sounds like a boon to the average taxpayer. But in fact they are slanted toward the wealthy. The $750 extra exemption for the elderly means $337.50 in the pocket of a man earning $40,000 a year and paying taxes in the 45-per-cent bracket; for the family living on $5000, the deduction amounts only to a $128.50 tax reduction. For the family earning $3000 and paying no federal income taxes at all, the deduction means nothing at all.

Deductions, incentives, and other ways of spending federal money by forgiving tax liabilities have had a special appeal to the Congress, including many liberal congressmen. Unlike direct federal expenditures, these "tax expenditures" do not appear in the budget and cannot easily be condemned as "reckless spending." The people whose taxes are forgiven are grateful; those whose taxes must eventually be raised will never know where to place the blame.

Aside from cosmetic advantage, tax deductions offer some procedural attractions to those frustrated by the Congressional committee system. Unlike direct government expenditures, tax expenditures do not have to negotiate the two-stage process of authorization and appropriations. Suppose, for example, that a congressman wants to have the federal government grant money to parents for their child-care expenses. The subsidy could be accomplished either through a direct federal grant program, or by permitting tax deductions for approved child-care expenses. But the first alternative would demand an authorizing measure, which would be sent to the education committees in the House and Senate, and a later money bill, which would have to clear both chambers' appropriations committees. A tax deduction need only travel through House Ways and Means and Senate Finance committees, or, in some cases, might even be adopted by direct vote from the floor without committee consideration.

In the late 1950s and 1960s, some Congressional liberals turned to "tax incentives" as a means for accomplishing the aims of the leftover New Deal agenda. (Conservatives had discovered the uses of the tax law long before.) Heralding a new era of partnership between business and government, liberal senators such as Jacob Javits, Abraham Ribicoff, and Robert Kennedy vied with each other in devising ambitious incentive schemes. By the end of the 1960s, tax provisions were on the books to encourage corporate investment (the Kennedy Administration's 7-per-cent credit), new low- and middle-income housing, pollution control, investment in less developed countries, foreign trade, and housing rehabilitation.

But tax deductions and incentives, while they bear the name of the liberals' traditional enthusiasms, accomplish few of their redistributive objectives. As former Treasury official Stanley Surrey has observed, the best way to gauge precisely who does benefit from tax expenditures is to rephrase them as equivalent programs of direct federal grants. For example, the deduction for charitable contributions can be reworded as a federal matching-grant program, which gives money to the favorite charities of private donors. Again, the grant schedule is peculiar. If a rich man gives $60 to charity, the government in effect writes a $140 check to the same cause. If a family earning $7500 a year gives $60 to its charity, the government's check only amounts to $22.29. If a $3500 family scrapes up $60, the government writes no check at all.

Other "tax expenditures" show the same bias. Tax relief for state- and municipal-bond interest costs the federal government about $2.3 billion a year and confers perhaps $1.6 billion in benefits to state and local governments in the form of reduced interest payments. The remaining $700 million is simply a subsidy to wealthy bondholders, who would otherwise be forced to pay taxes on the coupons. Federal tax benefits for homeowners amounted to an estimated $9.6 billion for 1972, dwarfing the $1.9-billion direct subsidy for low- and middle-income housing. The tax benefits were hugely regressive, conferring an average benefit of $3.55 on a family earning less than $5000 and an average of $1157 on the

$50,000 to $100,000 family. Over-all, the liberal acceptance of tax incentives resembles their reformulation of New Deal direct-expenditure programs—a half-conscious choice for political effectiveness at the expense of egalitarian principle.

In the late 1960s, for example, partisans of the War on Poverty combined with construction and banking interests to propose a new direction for government housing programs. In 1967, President Johnson appointed a committee on urban housing—headed by Edgar Kaiser, the very model of the high-minded industrialist beloved of the Great Society —which proposed an annual $5- to $6-billion program of tax subsidies and grants "to realize within a decade the goal of a decent home for every American." In 1968, Congress passed the Housing and Urban Development Act, billed by Johnson as the Magna Carta of housing and incorporating many of the Kaiser proposals for aid to apartment dwellers and the poor. Further subsidies were added by the (egregiously mistitled) Tax Reform Act of 1969.

But the new programs were targeted for the lower middle class rather than the poor: most of the housing went to families with annual incomes of $6000 to $10,000. Indeed, the real gainers were neither group, but rather the rich people who invested in tax-subsidized housing and the promoters who built it—in the words of Housing and Urban Development Secretary George Romney, "the fast-buck artists, the speculators, and the unscrupulous developers." Speaking in 1972, Romney added: "Reports have come back of new or 'rehabilitated' housing with leaky roofs, leaky plumbing, leaky basements, slipshod carpentry work, loose stair treads, paper-thin walls, inoperative furnaces and appliances, inadequate insulation, inferior wiring, and a whole host of complaints." Through its tax-subsidy program, the government had become committed to making payments on forty-year mortgages for buildings that would never last that long.

The waste and maldistribution of federal tax-subsidized housing are not peculiar to construction programs, but reflect a generic problem with tax expenditures. When a new tax incentive is proposed, there is rarely any careful calculation of costs and benefits. The basic judgment is simply that more should be spent, and that tax subsidies offer a politically convenient source of funds: we need more housing, so let's offer a tax break. But the same freedom from close scrutiny that commends tax expenditures as a political device virtually insures that they will cost too much and line the wrong pockets.

The cumulative impact of tax privileges has obliterated the progressive rates of the income tax. In 1971, a casual reader of tax schedules might have thought that the tax brackets ranged from 14 per cent up to 70 per cent, that a couple earning $65,000 would pay 35 per cent of their income in taxes while one earning $1 million would fork over 67 per cent. But, in fact, the average rate for taxpayers in the $50,000 to $75,000 range was 22 per cent; for those earning above $1 million, the average was only 32 per cent. For the vast majority of taxpayers, the federal income tax was only slightly progressive.

The Social Security payroll tax adds a further regressive bias to the federal tax system: since the tax only applies to earned income under a given maximum (most recently $9000) and not to higher earnings or to property income, it bears most heavily on the working poor. Nominally, employers pay a tax equal to that on employees; but the data suggest that this part of the tax simply reduces the employer's wage rates, and thus it too is borne by the worker. Over-all, the impact of federal taxes is simply proportional to income except for the most affluent 5 per cent of the population.

State and local taxes are sharply regressive for the very poor and roughly proportional for everyone else. Thus the net impact of all taxes combined is a small gain for the middle classes at the expense of the extremes. Taxes in this country are not, and never have been, a vehicle for significant redistribution.

Government spending does accomplish some redistribution, though in a far more limited way than liberals have imagined. The basic distinction is between straight payments which transfer money directly from the government —such as welfare and social security—and government programs designed to provide specific goods and services, such as schools, housing, and transportation. Transfer payments are indispensable aids for the very poor—families earning under $2000 a year in 1965 received more from government transfers than from all other sources. But transfers barely affect the distribution of income for the highest-earning 85 per cent of the population.

For other government programs the story is more complex. The largest item is primary and secondary education. If one makes the assumption that schools are worth what they cost, the poor gain substantially from state-provided education. But studies such as the Coleman report, an extensive statistical survey which found that the level of school expenditures made no difference on achievement-test scores, suggest a more skeptical appraisal. Similarly, one must be skeptical about the stated cost of programs like Medicaid and public housing which provide transfers of services and buildings to the poor. Segregated and substandard facilities and a lack of other options make these programs less valuable to their beneficiaries than an equivalent amount of cash; though they are, of course, considerably better than nothing.

Even more striking evidence concerns the programs central to the post-New Deal liberal strategy, such as subsidies for higher education. State-supported colleges and universities, although legally available to all, are used more than proportionately by the affluent. University of Wisconsin economists W. Lee Hansen and Burton A. Weisbrod have studied California's supposedly egalitarian system of colleges and universities. They found that students from poor families were the least likely to attend. Proportionately, six times as many high-school graduates from families earning over $25,000 planned to attend UC as did those whose parents earned less than $4000.

To be sure, all high-school graduates in California are eligible for two-year junior colleges. But the state subsidy for a student who completes state college or university is between four and five times that for a junior-college graduate. The net effect of free higher education, even in California, has been to channel the highest scholarships to the richest students.

Proposals to make the middle class pay directly for its services, rather than finance them through tax dollars, often run aground on opposition from liberal legislators and their professional-class supporters. A prime example is the Educational Opportunity Bank, a plan devised by Milton Friedman but endorsed by many economists of all political stripes. In its broadest version, suggested by James Tobin, the bank would offer every American at age eighteen a line of credit usable for any form of academic or vocational training. Loan repayment would be stretched out over the recipient's working life, with payments scaled to the borrower's income—for example, a student might agree to pay back 1 per cent of his income for every $2500 borrowed. The Wall Street lawyer would pay back more than he borrowed, the Lenox Avenue social worker less, but on the average the loan fund would break even. Unlike current loan programs, the Ed Bank would not saddle students with fixed interest charges and high repayments in the years immediately following graduation. But, over the course of their lifetimes, students as a class rather than parents or taxpayers would pay for the cost of their education.

Two Democratic governors have proposed limited versions of the Education Bank, and a few private universities have adopted its loan-payback scheme for their own use. But active opposition has come from the National Association of Land-Grant Colleges, an organization of tax-supported state universities, which fears that if loans took the place of tax subsidies in financing public universities, the best students would be lost to the private schools.

With the support of thousands of influential alumni active in local politics, and without the stigma of commercial self-interest, the education establishment is now one of the most powerful lobbies in Washington. When President Nixon proposed giving educational grants directly to students and letting them decide where to spend the money, the educators mustered their support among liberal Democrats and Northern Republicans for the competing principle of direct institutional grants, and won. Without ever having to face a fight, they have killed the Education Bank in committee.

The "new priorities" of the late 1960s and early 1970s may show an even more severe middle-class bias than subsidized university education. Current and proposed water-purification programs will cost tens of billions of dollars in tax money and higher product prices for modest improvements in rural streams and none at all in urban rivers where the poor might conceivably swim. Clean air will soothe the lungs of the poor as well as the rich, but it, too, will be financed through higher prices. Day-care centers may perform the genuine service of liberating housewives from boredom and subservience, but they will do so at a cost of perhaps $2000 per child per year; if the burden is placed on the tax system, it is the less affluent who will pay.

For many other public programs the results are comparable. Federal agricultural programs notoriously favor the large farmer: the highest-earning 20 per cent of beneficiaries receive 93 per cent of the subsidies for cotton, 96 per cent for sugar, and probably about 70 or 80 per cent for price-support programs as a whole. The lowest-income fifth of the nation's farmers, on the other hand, garner only about one twentieth of the total subsidy.

The federal government's transportation programs tell a similar story of favoritism, in this case to special interests. In 1960, the budget contained about $270 million in subsidies to maintain a hugely inefficient merchant marine, $500 million to aid airlines and private plane-owners, and precisely $0 for mass transit. By fiscal year 1972, priorities had shifted a bit: urban mass transit now received $327 million, while aviation was up to $2 billion; the merchant marine, designed to safeguard the United States should World War II break out again, extracted an additional half billion dollars.

It would be comfortable to ascribe these failings not to the liberal programs themselves, but to their perversion by "the interests." Our plutocratic system of campaign financing, the seniority system in Congress, and the pervasive influence of corporate power have, of course, done their share to thwart redistribution. But the obstacle is more fundamental. Postwar government programs have been designed to benefit a vast middle-class constituency—largely, but not entirely, because the middle class has the votes. Beyond short-run political calculation, liberals have an ideological commitment to the extension of the public sector. Health, housing, and education programs for the middle class are regarded as a good thing in themselves, without close questioning as to who pays the bills. At times a little rationalizing terminology is in order. Writing in 1969, Arthur Schlesinger, Jr., spoke of the new "qualitative liberalism" that was replacing the old economic concerns for the underprivileged: "Quantitative liberalism appealed to those of low income; qualitative liberalism appealed to those of high education. The level of education has become increasingly the dividing line of the politics of the sixties as economic issues began to yield to moral and cultural issues." By defining subsidized middle-class amenities as "qualitative," liberals have masked the unpleasant facts about distribution.

This attitude toward the public sector is not limited to American liberals, but characterizes the European left as well. The redistributive failure of the British Labour Party, for example, derives from much of the same ideology that guides American liberals. A glance at Britain suggests the difficulties which an egalitarian policy of our own would have to overcome.

During the 1950s, writers on both the left and the right assumed that wartime taxation and postwar Labour rule had accomplished a major leveling of incomes. New and expanded social services—especially the National Health Service—supposedly concentrated their benefits upon the poor. Full employment steadily compressed wage and salary differentials. Stiff estate taxes forced the hereditary rich to move off of their manors and live off of their capital. High professional incomes were eroded as Harley Street made way for the national health and the Inns of Court ran up against the income tax.

Both legislation and ideology in postwar Britain were shaped by this assumption of increasing equality. Regressive new taxes gained support on the premise that the shift toward equality had gone about as far as it could go. This was so far, argued Labour revisionist Anthony Crosland, that Britain could no longer be considered a capitalist state. With the perquisites of ownership so diminished by government ownership and regulation, and with equality of incomes so nearly attained, Crosland believed that Labour should free itself of the nomenclature and preoccupations of the old-fashioned class struggle.

The task for Labour, instead, was but to complete the construction of socialism. To be sure, for many right-wing Labourites "socialism" was simply a monicker for a Galbraithian mixed economy featuring private ownership heavily doused with government planning. But the left wing of the party had a more heroic vision in mind. Socialism, to Aneurin Bevan, Michael Foot, and their brethren on the Labour left, meant nationalization of at least transport, communications, banking, and large segments of heavy industry. Even more immediately, it meant an end to the "means test"—the practice of confining government-provided social services to the poor. Social services, the left argued, should be freely available to all.

The left-wing obsession with the means test was founded on both humane principle and political calculation. The means test, Peter Townsend recently wrote in a Fabian pamphlet, "fosters hierarchical relationships of superiority and inferiority in society, diminishes rather than enhances the status of the poor, and has the effect of widening rather than reducing social inequalities." Excluding the middle class from social services "distracts attention from the problem of improving [their] quality" and increasing their budgets. Conversely, by blanketing the middle class into one key social service—National Health—Labourites felt they had guaranteed the permanence of socialized medicine and assured a minimum standard of care for the poor. More generally, left-wing Labourites argued that the means test betokened an accepting anti-Socialist attitude toward the machinery of the capitalist state: "[it assumes] that the circumstances of the poor can be greatly improved without changing major social institutions and severely limiting the opportunity of the prosperous sections of the population to accumulate more privileges." If, on the contrary, social programs were extended to all, the groundwork would be laid for that "complex reconstruction of the systems of reward in society" which would truly spell socialism.

When Labour has been in power, the left's enthusiasm for "universality" in social services has had to confront the exigencies of the Exchequer. Universal services are expensive services; faced with pressure on the pound and taxpayer discontent, Labour governments have had to compromise with their opposition in principle to the means test. In 1951, the Attlee government imposed charges on National Health dentures and spectacles, leading to the resignation of Health Minister Bevan and others of his faction, including at the time the young Harold Wilson. When an older and more malleable Wilson was Prime Minister in the 1960s, his pledges for expanded school construction, university grants, and lower National Health charges had to be put aside in the interests of another embattled defense of the pound. But Labour's imperfect record in practice has not diminished its formal commitment to universality.

What explains the failure of egalitarian policy in both Great Britain and the United States? Much of the blame lies with the liberal planners and their overambitious multiplicity of goals. Liberals have believed not merely in redistribution, but in the inherent desirability of a large public sector, in free and universal access to the social services, and in the use of tax exemptions for social purposes. The result has been to multiply the burden on the income tax while shrinking its base. "We have traveled down the vicious path of decadent tax systems," observed the Labour economist Nicholas Kaldor, "the path of charging more and more on less and less."

As the income tax became overloaded and unpopular, liberal politicians in America, like Labourites in Britain, turned to regressive payroll and consumption taxes to pay for the welfare state. Britain financed her system of old-age pensions by imposing a head tax—the most regressive tax of all. Harold Wilson's initiatives in education and housing were paid for by higher sales taxes on beer and cigarettes. A respectable case can be made that the poor grew poorer under the most recent Labour government.

Adoption of proposals for universal health insurance in the United States will compound the burden of the regressive payroll tax and increase pressure for a national sales tax. Already such a tax may be in the works. The European Common Market is moving toward a uniform "value added tax," probably at a rate approximating 20 per cent, to supplant already operating VATs in most member nations. The VAT is applied to goods at each stage of the process of production and distribution—on an automobile, for example, the tax is first paid by the companies that mine the minerals that go into steel, then by the steel manufacturer and fabricator, next by the auto manufacturer, and finally by the retailer. At each step, the tax is paid on the difference between the value of the components coming into the firm and the value going out—in other words, on the "value added" at that stage. The result is essentially a hidden sales tax, concealed in the price of the final product.

The VAT has received favorable scrutiny by members of the Nixon Administration and is widely expected to be part of a proposal for reducing the role of the property tax in financing public education. But, once adopted, the VAT would quickly be put to other uses as well. It would provide a relatively easy means for the expansion of federal revenues and the further erosion of progressive taxation. The visible, complicated income tax could rapidly give way to a concealed levy on consumption as the federal government's main source of revenue.

It would be unfair simply to blame liberal ideology for the defeat of income redistribution. Much of what the left did was thought to be politically unavoidable. Labour and the Democrats did need middle-class votes; the price they necessarily paid was middle-class programs. Tax benefits for home-ownership and Social Security pensions that vary inversely with need have, as intended, helped to ensure the permanence of New Deal legislation and of Democratic Congressional majorities. In this explanation, however, lies a refutation of Galbraith. The public sector, rather than serving to camouflage an unpopular program of equality, has simply hidden from liberals the evidence of their willingness to ally themselves with the more prosperous and to abandon the poor.

In the 1950s, liberal enthusiasm for public spending probably did not thwart redistribution, since major political forces were in fact unwilling to bring pressure for it. Galbraith accurately summarized the political stalemate on equality. But more recently, the War on Poverty, the collapse of the welfare system, and the growing militancy of the poor themselves have given legitimacy to proposals for a negative income tax. Some form of explicit redistribution— probably the Nixon Administration's diminutive Family Assistance Plan—seems likely to be adopted someday.

The constraint at present is as much financial as ideological. Even a half-hearted negative income tax would have an enormous cost. Providing a minimum $3600 income for a family of four would add $25 billion to the federal budget; a $5500 plan would cost $71 billion.

These sums are not about to be voted by today's Congress. But the amount that will be available depends, in large part, on other claims on the federal budget. Theoretically, room could be found for an adequate negative income tax by lopping off the most wasteful and destructive parts of the budget, such as excess defense spending and road building. The United States could defend herself on $20 billion less per year. Additional funds—Joseph Pechman estimates over $25 billion—could be raised through federal tax reform. But, in actuality, liberals have never had the votes to squeeze $10 billion from these sources, much less $30 or $60 billion.

Funds of this magnitude will be raised, if at all, only at the expense of traditional liberal enthusiasms. To accomplish any significant redistribution of income, liberals would have to abandon their ambitions for universal health insurance, generous urban aid, and huge housing subsidies. Conceivably, this reorientation is possible. But a far more likely scenario would simply extend the experience of the last two decades. The federal budget would expand, meeting the perceived needs of the middle class and retreating further from progressive taxation. Programs advocated in the name of Franklin Roosevelt would be devoted to the goals of Nelson Rockefeller. The public sector would serve the poor with one hand and tax them with the other. The role of the vast majority of urban blacks would then be as stated by Daniel Patrick Moynihan, addressing President-elect Nixon not about this generation but about the next one: "They are not going to become capitalists, nor even middle-class functionaries. But it is fully reasonable to conceive of them being transformed into a stable working-class population: truck drivers, mail carriers, assemblyline workers—people with dignity, purpose, and in the United States a very good standard of living indeed."

Real progress will depend, as ever before, on economic growth.

II

Objections to the Economic Side Effects of Growth

3

The New Economics and
the Old Shibboleths:
A Short History

In the late 1950s, Nikita Khrushchev announced that he would bury us; under an avalanche of toasters and television sets, he later elaborated. Russia's growth rate was then 6.5 per cent; ours was 2.3 per cent. At that pace, Russia would drown us in milk production by the mid-1960s and overtake our GNP by 1979.

Americans took heed. The 1960 Democratic convention announced a target growth rate of 5 per cent, delaying Russia's projected triumph until 2014. Candidate John F. Kennedy promised "to get this country moving again." For a while, stepped-up economic growth was the official and uncontested aim of national policy.

More than a decade later, growth has become almost as passé as the Cold War rhetoric which gave it prominence.

No one worries about Russia's growth rate and few about our own. The Kennedy Administration's fretful watch over GNP, like its obsession with national prestige, strikes most of us as a neurotic aberration of a vanished era.

Why, during those ten years, did we lose our commitment to growth? The answer lies only partly in our doubts about the virtues of materialism. To be sure, the new sensitivities about the environment, wasteful consumption, and economic imperialism have had their influence. But the arguments most decisive in hampering growth have been present for twenty or thirty years and were only temporarily submerged during the 1960s. Central to these arguments was a quarrel, not with the goal of prosperity, but with the means necessary to attain it.

High-growth policies are "full throttle" policies. They require expansion of the economy so that it operates at full capacity, without idle machines and workless men. Full employment inspires businesses to new investment; and investment, as Galbraith puts it, "is what nurtures growth." But uninhibited expansion of the economy rouses opposition from those who fear it will lead to economic chaos. The specter takes many forms—rampant inflation, which evaporates hard-earned savings and pension rights; balance-of-payments losses, which leave the government an embarrassed debtor to the nations of the world; budget deficits, which must be added to the awesome national debt. One or another of these fears has kept America's postwar economic managers from pursuing their avowed goal of full employment and steady growth.

Growth was not recognized as a public issue until Sputnik went into orbit, but its twin, full employment, has been prime political fare since the end of World War II.* For politicians in the late 1940s, the main objection to full-employment policies was their link with the mysterious arts of John Maynard Keynes. Keynes had written his *General Theory of Employment, Money and Interest* in 1936, expecting it to revolutionize economic thought within ten years. He beat his schedule. By the early 1940s, Keynesian theories had penetrated American universities and shaped the outlook of at least some Democrats and liberals on the major economic questions of the day.

The crux of Keynes's message was that depressions do not cure themselves. Modern industrial economies were not automatically guaranteed the promised land of high employment and steady growth. Smart and timely government intervention, Keynes argued, was needed to head off sharp swings in the business cycle. For slumps, the cure was to increase purchasing power by reducing taxes or injecting government spending. More money to spend would mean more demand for goods. The result would be new jobs and a stimulus for businessmen to open new plants and buy new machinery. If the recession were not too severe, the same end could also be achieved by cutting interest rates and making it cheaper for corporations to borrow.

The boom end of the cycle, Keynes wrote, could be

---

* Here we are treating two issues together—growth and full employment—which are in theory distinct. It is at least conceivable that one could have speedy growth without full employment—we could imagine an economy in which the machinery of production grew rapidly while men eager to work were turned away at the factory gates. But, in practice, the policies that promote growth of economic capacity through private investment also lead to high employment. Fiscal and monetary expansion simultaneously spur growth through increased investment, and boost employment by giving businesses an incentive to hire more workers.

The New Economics and the Old Shibboleths   93

calmed either by hiking taxes, slimming government expenditures, or raising interest rates charged to business. Higher taxes would cut into the take-home pay of workers and the net profits of business, thereby limiting the demand for goods, while a cut in the government budget would also reduce pressure on the economy by freeing up resources for private consumption. Steeper interest rates would force corporations to put off their investment projects. Any of the three could accomplish the same goal—the reduction of inflationary pressure caused by too much money chasing too few goods.

Conservative politicians had several kinds of objections to Keynesianism. Some simply did not understand or would not listen: Keynes was an English snob who had made a career of attacking accepted doctrines of every sort. And his haughty Oxbridge manners did not win him friends in provincial Washington.

But for many conservatives the complaint was more profound. Keynesian theories implied the need for an active, flexible public sector: the government could not simply run the post office, make war, and otherwise mind its own business. "Social planners" would dictate the rise and fall of federal revenues and expenditures as a device to smooth the business cycle. In contrast, the old-fashioned prescription for balanced budgets—which Keynes would throw out the window—made real political sense to conservatives. If new tax revenues had to be found to finance new government activities, there would be some check on creeping socialism. People would be forced to face the fact that you couldn't get something for nothing. But if the government was *supposed* to spend more than it taxed to end a recession, there would be no bound to statist schemes.

Aside from this strategic fondness for restraints on big government, conservatives sincerely believed that a balanced budget and a low public debt were the twin pillars of prosperity: "I don't think you can spend yourself rich," observed Eisenhower's Treasury Secretary, George Humphrey, when asked whether government expenditures should be used to fight a recession. "I think we went through all that for a good many years and we kept spending, and spending and spending, and we still didn't help our employment or help our total position."

Fears of national bankruptcy clouded the horizons of the opponents of federal deficits the way the threat of debtors' prison disciplined Mr. Micawber to the prudent life. Eisenhower feared the "burden of the [public] debt on our grandchildren" and believed that "continued deficit spending is immoral." The Keynesian rebuttal—that the national debt is harmless because we owe it to ourselves—lacked sufficient resemblance to common sense to be convincing. No business-executive-turned-politician could easily make the transition from the rules of the corporate balance sheet to the unintuitive mysteries of public finance.

In the immediate postwar period, these objections to Keynesianism were overridden by memories of bread lines of the 1930s. Many economists expected World War II to be succeeded by a second world depression, or at least a stiff recession. Recessions had followed wars in the past, and now there was scientific reason as well as precedent to anticipate bad times.

A group of American disciples of Keynes, led by Harvard's Alvin Hansen, expanded on the prophet's words by predicting that America was headed for long-term stagnation that had only been postponed by the war. A rich nation, they claimed, would spend too little of its income to use all of its productive capacity. The modern industrial economy, if left on its own, would be permanently plagued by insufficient purchasing power. Only constant government intervention through spending programs and tax cuts could keep the economy employed and growing. Influenced by the American Keynesians, Congress in 1946 passed the Full Employment Act, which made "maximum employment, production, and purchasing power" explicit goals of government policy and directed the President to propose appropriate measures. Signing the law, President Harry S. Truman called it "a commitment to take any and all of the measures necessary for a healthy economy."

Although gaining acceptance in principle, Keynesian methods had little immediate occasion to be tried out in practice. For several years there was no recession to fight. The prediction of stagnation was discredited. Quite the opposite case, the problem of inflationary pressures on the economy, became the major concern. Everybody was busy buying things—cars, homes, and, eventually, television sets. Inflation was regarded as a hangover from the removal of wartime price controls and from the temporary impact of consumer desires pent up by wartime scarcity. It would (and did) cure itself; Truman's request for continued controls fell on deaf Congressional ears. When a mild recession finally did come in 1949, the downturn reversed itself in short order and was followed by brisk expansion after the outbreak of the Korean War.

Postwar prosperity quickly had its influence on America's economic ideology. For conservatives, it reaffirmed their distrust of Keynesianism: the professors peddling the new economics had been wrong after all. There was no depression, hence no need to gear up the government for intervention in the economy. History seemed to have vindicated conservative economists such as George Terborgh, who asserted that "seldom has so pretentious a body of doctrine been so scantily fortified by factual evidence."

Liberals did not repudiate the new Keynesian ideas (quite properly, since it was only Hansen's predictions of stagnation and not Keynes's analysis of the effect of government intervention that had been shown wrong). But they did escape from their Depression gloom. By the early 1950s, liberal writers were hailing a commonwealth of permanent plenty with goods and services for all. Briefly, liberals serenaded growth as both desirable and inevitable—the fulfillment of the American Dream, the free world's answer to communism.

But some had second thoughts. They remained sure that prosperity was the wave of the future (thanks to Keynes), but began to doubt its worth. Beneath the surface Babbittry of the 1950s there grew an influential disquiet. Liberal sociologists bemoaned the "lonely crowd," while the movie studios chronicled the woes of unsatisfied men in gray flannel suits. Suburbia was seen as the home of organization men who had traded their identity for second cars. The lesson was that American prosperity was false, shallow, or in any event no panacea for the enduring problems of human existence.

John Kenneth Galbraith refined and distributed one version of this message in his 1958 book, *The Affluent Society*. Galbraith argued that economic growth in America led to a chronic deficiency of public amenities, a condition which Galbraith termed "social imbalance."

The family that takes its mauve and cerise, air-conditioned, power-steered, and power-braked car out for a tour passes through cities that are badly paved, made hideous by litter, blighted by buildings, billboards, and posts for wires that should long since have been put underground. . . . They picnic on exquisitely packaged food from a portable icebox by a polluted stream and go on to spend the night at a park which is a menace to public health and morals. Just before dozing off on an air mattress, beneath a nylon tent, amid the stench of decaying refuse, they may vaguely reflect on the curious unevenness of their blessings.

With spokesmen like Galbraith fretting the problems of abundance, the liberals were poorly disposed to man the barricades for growth. The slow-growth years of the Eisenhower Administration, with their economic surges punctuated by three recessions in the familiar stop-go pattern of pre-Keynesian times, drew some sharp attacks from Democrats (including Galbraith). But the academic liberals, the refiners of Keynesian economics, never formulated a coherent, politically appealing policy of growth. The attacks on empty American materialism diluted their devotion to growth and left the business of managing prosperity to the Republicans. Galbraith had never argued for a halt to growth—in fact, he had proposed its acceleration. But the most biting part of his message, the hoggish quality of American consumption, insulated the Republican no-growth record from one prime basis for criticism.

For the bankers, corporation executives, and conservative economists who ran the Eisenhower Administration, affluence posed no moral dilemma. They worshiped the GNP in principle and stunted it only in practice. Treasury Secretary George Humphrey and Budget Director Maurice Stans had no objections to tail fins and power steering. But they could not abide federal spending. To the Republicans, the Keynesian methods that alone could produce growth were still works of a Socialist devil.

If creeping socialism made spending *verboten,* the Republicans could still have used tax cuts to bolster employment and growth. And Eisenhower never explicitly closed the door to government intervention, given sufficient need: "At the first sign of approaching recession in this country, there will be instantly mobilized . . . every resource . . . of the federal government to see that never again shall depression come to us." However, his fundamental priority was laid down in 'a message to Congress just two weeks after he took office: "The first order of business," Eisenhower announced, "is the elimination of the annual deficit." At one point the President confided to his Cabinet (in the words of his aide, Sherman Adams) "that if he was able to do nothing as President except balance the budget, he would feel that his time in the White House was well spent."

The mildest of tax cuts—a Republican-sponsored $1-billion reduction in excise revenues—was in fact passed by Congress in response to the post-Korea downturn of 1954. But the measure never had Administration backing, largely due to George Humphrey's opposition to deficit spending. Tax reduction sacrificed the principle of the balanced budget, a precept only slightly less important than the principle of as little government as possible. Humphrey thought that the recession was only an innocuous "rolling readjustment"; others in the White House liked to call it a "sideslip." Defense Secretary Charles Wilson spoke his mind on unemployment (he'd "always liked bird dogs better than kennel-fed dogs. . . . You know, one who'd get out and hunt for his food rather than sit on his fanny and yell"), and the Democrats won a fat midterm victory.

Indeed, splits within the Cabinet on the priority to be given budget balancing may have fatally weakened support for the Administration's own fiscal program for cutting business taxes. Without any Keynesian intent, the program was designed to encourage long-term investment through special tax incentives. But the program would have had the embarrassing feature of a Keynesian-like revenue reduction of $1.4 billion in fiscal 1955, piled on top of the projected federal deficit.

The easy recovery from the 1954 recession—unemployment fell below 4 per cent by midyear—did little to discredit the Administration's taboo on deficit spending. "Instead of expanding federal enterprises or initiating new spending programs," bragged Eisenhower in his 1955 economic report, "the basic policy of the Government in dealing with the contraction was to take actions that created confidence in the future. . . ." And in that future the aim was to be "fostering long-term growth" rather than "imparting an immediate upward thrust" to the nation's economy. Later in 1955, when the Senate turned down a House-passed tax cut, Eisenhower asked reporters, "Would it be allowable just to say hurrah?"

Economic recovery (still accompanied by substantial unemployment) was met with plans for budget surpluses in the fiscal years 1956 and 1957. The weak voices that had promoted active intervention in the 1954 recession, led by the chairman of the Council of Economic Advisers, Arthur Burns, were entirely dominated by Eisenhower's anguish over possible inflation. In 1957, Eisenhower's hardly expansionary budget was denounced by his own Treasury Secre-

tary (its high spending, said George Humphrey, would cause
" a depression that will curl your hair"). Eisenhower meekly
announced that he had approved Humphrey's remarks and
sat back to watch Congress wield the knife.

Although spending was being held down, tax cuts were seriously pondered after the economy took an alarming downturn in the fall of 1957. Even the Chamber of Commerce
recognized that the nation had entered the "biggest recession
since World War II." By April 1958, unemployment had
reached 7.5 per cent—a postwar record—and a vocal Administration faction led by Burns and Vice-President Richard M. Nixon campaigned for lower taxes. They were joined
by elite business leaders in the Committee for Economic Development and rank-and-file captains of industry in the
Chamber of Commerce, more interested in profits than ideological purity. But the President remained skeptical: "Well,
of course, this has been argued pro and con. Mr. Baruch said
yesterday that he couldn't think of anything being greater
folly than a general tax cut. I believe there are factors on
each side of this business."

The Administration's hesitation to take action in spite of
7-per-cent unemployment and an impending Congressional
election cannot be entirely explained by a devotion to the
catechism of the balanced budget. The President was
plagued with worries about inflation. Recent experience suggested that the economy would lean toward inflation even
when it wasn't operating at full capacity. Full employment
and high growth would only make things worse. Even a tax
cut designed merely to end the recession would lead to inflationary pressures once recovery set in. And, reasoned Eisenhower, politicians wouldn't have the nerve to restore the old,
higher tax rates to combat rising prices. Better, he con-

cluded, to avoid a tax cut now than to face runaway inflation later.

Even some of the businessmen who favored a tax cut were impressed by this hazard. Theodore Yntema, vice-president of Ford Motor, argued that "once the public discovers how effective mass tax reduction is, there will be a temptation to use it whenever unemployment rises to 3 or 4 per cent instead of when it reaches 7 per cent. If we use such measures when unemployment is only 3 or 4 per cent, we shall reap the whirlwind of inflation."

Eisenhower finally rejected the proposal for a tax cut and was rewarded with a spontaneous upswing in output. Thus fortified, the Administration could once more indulge its fiscal conservatism. It moved swiftly to wipe out the increased debt that had been built up because of low tax revenues during the recession. The year 1959 passed with the Federal Reserve Board tightening money and the Administration choking the budget. Ruinous inflation and an unsound dollar, warned the President once more, awaited any deviation from its ascetic course. Symbolically, Eisenhower asked Congress to amend the 1946 Full Employment Act so that "reasonable price stability" could be added to its litany of goals.

Aside from inflation worries, Eisenhower was deeply troubled by the deteriorating balance of payments, the difference between what America spends abroad and what she takes in. In the first postwar decade, the United States had been free from payments troubles, thanks to her ability to sell consumer goods and investment equipment to the war-shocked European economies. As George Humphrey put it, "We've been making the automobiles and farm machinery and everything else and selling them all over the world." But with European recovery there began a steady erosion of the U.S. payments balance. Revenues from our cars and everything else were no longer sufficient to cover mounting U.S. tourist and military spending abroad. More and more dollars were piling up in the hands of foreigners, and in 1958–1959 three billion of those dollars were cashed in for gold.

For Eisenhower, the decisive balance-of-payments event was the return of Treasury Secretary Robert Anderson from the New Delhi meetings of the World Bank and the International Monetary Fund. "In their corridor conversations," reports Charles Silberman, "Anderson had heard central bankers from all over the world questioning the soundness of the dollar. . . ." These rumblings gave Anderson "the shock of my life." Eisenhower reverberated in tune. The Administration resolved to cut the budget, recession or no. "There was not a night," said Budget Director Maurice Stans, "that I didn't go home and brood over the human, the social, and the security aspects of the decisions that were taking form. I found myself wondering whether I was being too hidebound in my political philosophy. But in my thinking I always came back to one conclusion: In fiscal matters there is no tolerable alternative to conservatism. There is a discipline here that can be ignored only at the peril of the nation's organized life."

Continuing this "discipline," Eisenhower's budget for fiscal year 1961—presented in January 1960—called for a major surplus at a time when the economy was wallowing near 6-per-cent unemployment. In February 1960, Arthur Burns predicted that this severely constricted budget would stymie the recovery. Once more, Burns urged fiscal expansion; again he was backed by Richard Nixon, this time with a special urgency. As Nixon later remarked in *Six*

Crises: "In October, usually a month of rising employment, the jobless rolls increased by 452,000. All the speeches, television broadcasts and precinct work could not counteract that one hard fact." A stronger economy would almost surely have made Nixon President.

The result of Eisenhower economics was stagnation. Per-capita income grew only 1 per cent annually during the Eisenhower years, compared with 2 per cent during the preceding five years and 4 per cent in the next five. In each of the three recessions of the Eisenhower Administration, fears of inflation, federal deficits, and world disenchantment with the dollar had subdued the desire for economic growth. Cyclical decline was met with soul-searching inactivity, while cyclical recovery was choked off by budget surpluses in the name of fiscal responsibility. "We tightened more than we needed in terms of production and employment," recalled Henry Wallich, a member of the Council of Economic Advisers, "but not more than we needed in terms of prices and the balance of payments. It had to be done, but it was done at a cost the magnitude of which wasn't realized at the time."

The language, and some of the obsessions, of Eisenhower's antigrowth policy were pre-Keynesian; and this aspect was less visible with the new Kennedy Administration. No New Frontiersman really believed that deficit spending was sinful, though Kennedy himself was terrified by its political consequences. Nor did the Democratic economists think that the public debt was a burden to their grandchildren or anyone else's. But in other respects their concerns were strikingly similar to Eisenhower's. Conservative arguments that defeated growth in the 1950s reappeared, with better syntax and more measured application, in the Democratic Administrations of the 1960s.

In the light of the 1960 election rhetoric, more active intervention in the economy by the new Administration would not have been surprising. The campaign had been dominated by Kennedy's promise to "get this country moving again"—as much to match the Soviet Union's victories in outer space and Cuba as to get the unemployed back to work. Kennedy's State of the Union message proclaimed that "the American economy is in trouble" and bemoaned "seven months of recession, three and one-half years of slack, seven years of diminished economic growth and nine years of falling farm income." The political virtues of fulfilling Kennedy's promise of growth were self-evident. What really requires explanation is how timidly Kennedy acted to restore full employment under the circumstances.

The initial Kennedy economic proposals consisted of a $3- to $5-billion increase in federal expenditures and a reshuffling of business taxes to encourage investment in plant and equipment. The budget increase was motivated more by the President's tough stand on Berlin, which prompted higher military spending, than by the need for fiscal stimulation; in fact, his economic advisers had to dissuade the President from proposing a $3-billion increase in income taxes. While the business-tax package contained a provision for cash credits against new investment expenditure, the expansionary effect was negated by increased tax revenues from other business sources. As a counter to 7-per-cent unemployment and $50 billion of idle capacity, Kennedy's approach was not much more aggressive than his predecessor's.

Eisenhower's reluctance to apply Keynesian methods has been explained easily enough. But for Kennedy, the problem was not ideological. Early Kennedy economics was the economics of how to get elected and stay elected, and it was unclear what political approach was indicated in 1961. JFK had run on a platform which promised balanced budgets as well as growth, and he had not hesitated to use the 1958 budget deficit against Nixon as a campaign issue. His appointment of C. Douglas Dillon, a Republican Wall Street banker who had voted for Nixon in 1960, to the Treasury was an indication of how cautiously he planned to act.

But a component of Kennedy conservatism was based on technical arguments at least compatible with Keynesianism: the policies of rapid growth meant a deterioration of the U.S. balance of payments. An increased pace of economic activity was well known to boost consumption of imported goods and decrease the exports needed to pay for them. Prosperity means more Porsches and vacations in Curaçao and it also means reduced incentives for American firms to set aside output for sales abroad. To sharpen the dilemma further, a policy of low interest rates designed to encourage domestic investment in new capital equipment also means an additional outflow of dollars to foreign security markets. Low interest rates in the United States drive dollars abroad in search of more profitable securities and reduce the foreign demand for securities in New York. Hence the net impact of American prosperity is more dollars going abroad and fewer coming back—a worsening of the balance of payments.

This dollar drain as a side effect of Keynesian expansion was particularly unwelcome to Kennedy in 1961. The accumulation of exchange deficits left the United States potentially vulnerable to a run on the dollar, in which foreigners would trade in their dollars for the gold in Fort Knox. Such a crisis became more likely as the foreign dollar claims grew while U.S. gold reserves dwindled. Kennedy feared the crisis would not only disrupt world trade and international investment but, worse yet, would tarnish America's prestige—a major preoccupation during the period.

The exact impact of the balance-of-payments argument on Kennedy's policies is not clear. Keynesian economists wanted to try an approach to the problem which would not sacrifice domestic prosperity. They advocated a combination of high interest rates to bring the dollars home, and very expansionary fiscal policy to counter the dampening effect of high interest rates on private investment. In theory, there was a mix of tight money, tax relief, and government spending which could restore full employment without jeopardizing the balance of payments. More importantly, the New Frontier economists wanted the United States to propose a fundamental reform of the world's monetary system, one designed to reduce the conflict between the domestic goal of rapid growth and the international objective of a "strong dollar" and balance-of-payments equilibrium.

But this approach was not easy to apply in practice. The Democrats had made a platform commitment to low interest rates as a sop to Populist elements in the party. Moreover, savings and loan associations and the construction industry, sources of major Democratic support, had no use for tight money. High interest rates meant fewer mortgages issued and fewer buildings built. For that matter, JFK could not dictate the course of interest rates. The tools of monetary policy are controlled by the Federal Reserve Board, whose membership is appointed to long terms that overlap the election of Presidents. Any program of fiscal and monetary policy Kennedy chose required the cooperation of the Fed.

Recognition of the balance-of-payments dilemma also left expansionary fiscal programs more vulnerable to conservative attack. The traditional banker's solution to payments deficits is slowing down the economy. And historian James Heath notes that this editorial tack was taken by both *The Wall Street Journal* and *The American Banker:* "Business placed greatest emphasis on the need for maintaining the soundness and integrity of the dollar. To achieve this goal Kennedy was urged to make a determined effort to balance the budget through vigorous pruning of nonessential government programs."

Kennedy himself strongly felt this pressure for economic orthodoxy. "I know everyone thinks I worry about this too much," Kennedy once told Theodore Sorensen, apropos of receiving yet another memo on the balance of payments, "but if there's ever a run on the bank, and I have to devalue the dollar or bring home our troops, as the British did, I'm the one who will take the heat. Besides it's a club that De Gaulle and all the others hang over my head. Any time there's a crisis or a quarrel, they can cash in all their dollars and where are we?"

The years 1961–1962 reproduced the Eisenhower pattern of weak gestures toward reviving the depressed economy followed by retrenchment after the recession had cured itself. Unemployment dipped below 6 per cent early in 1962 and, not coincidentally, Kennedy retreated from Keynesian talk. The President proposed a budget surplus for fiscal 1963. To complete the pattern, Kennedy justified his new budget with another Eisenhower preoccupation: "To plan a deficit under such circumstances would increase the risk of inflationary pressures, damaging . . . to our domestic economy."

Under the impact of "fiscal responsibility" expansion leveled off in the spring of 1962, leaving 5.5 per cent of the work force unemployed. Late in May, Wall Street, ulcerous over the steel-price confrontation and anticipating the first

Kennedy recession, reacted with a sharp sell-off of stocks. Kennedy's well-publicized assessment of the nation's men of industry ("My father always told me that all businessmen were sons-of-bitches, but I never believed him until now") only made matters worse. Things fell apart and the 680 Dow-Jones support level did not hold.

But antigrowth policies had more vigorous opponents in 1962 than they did in 1955, 1958, or 1960. Where Arthur Burns had cautiously counseled expansion against the bias of his experience and training, the New Frontier economists were committed to Keynesian solutions to unemployment. And where Eisenhower had been predisposed to accept Bernard Baruch's advice, Kennedy respected the economic and political wisdom of the professoriat. In early June, JFK's break with the past became clear. At Yale he argued,

> What is at stake in our economic decisions today is not some grand warfare of rival ideologies which will sweep the country with passion but the practical management of a modern economy. What we need are not labels and clichés, but more basic discussion of the sophisticated and technical questions involved in keeping a great economic machinery moving ahead. . . . I am suggesting that the problems of fiscal and monetary policy in the sixties . . . demand subtle challenges for which technical answers—not political answers—must be provided.

Kennedy called for a tax cut.

The revolution of the New Economics has been sufficiently chronicled to eliminate the need for a detailed recounting in these pages. Twenty months went by before the tax-cut proposal was signed into law in 1964. The time lapse was the result not simply of the power of conservative opposition but of the controversy over who was to reap the direct benefits of tax reduction. In its initial form the tax bill was linked to tax reform, and the special-interest lobbyists blocked enactment. However, by late 1963, tax reform had effectively been eliminated, and the remaining opposition settled for a token ceiling on federal expenditures as the price of passage.

The tax cut was clearly a triumph for the proponents of rapid economic growth. It added $36 billion to output and eliminated much of the "fiscal drag" on expansionary forces which had plagued each of the Eisenhower recoveries. Indeed, from the trough of the 1960–1961 recession through the Johnson years, output grew without pause at an annual rate averaging more than 4 per cent. But the use of fiscal policy to bring the economy to full employment was more a tactical victory for progrowth forces than a vanquishment of the opposition. The issue of the balanced budget was virtually eliminated.

However, many of the arguments against growth were simply left to simmer in the background. Worries about inflation did lead the Administration to promulgate voluntary wage and price "guideposts," intended to dissuade unions and management from excessive avarice. But no real choice had to be made between growth and inflation in 1964—the discipline of a decade of stagnation and $30 billion in excess economic capacity produced relatively stable prices. In the early Kennedy years, the cost of living rose about 1 per cent annually with only a modest acceleration thereafter. As Arthur Okun, President Johnson's CEA chairman, observed, "It was no surprise to find a departure from the virtually absolute stability of . . . wholesale prices that had ruled in earlier years. . . . [But] this was not inflation by any definition I know."

The balance-of-payments questions was temporarily neutralized as a pressing political issue by special restrictions on overseas investments and a determined effort to downgrade the importance of the problem. A new tax reduced incentives for Americans to buy foreign stocks and bonds. The value of goods tourists could bring in duty-free from abroad was slashed from $500 to $100. ("If we're restricting servicemen," the President said privately, "I don't see why these rich ——— can't do with a little less, including my sisters.") A Kennedy-appointed study commission recommended a change in the payments-accounting system to reduce the psychological burden of our debt to foreigners, much in the way that accountants manipulate corporation annual reports to look better in lean years. A bevy of envoys was sent to Europe to persuade our allies to change their dollar holdings into special bonds which would be a less visible threat to American "solvency."

Within the Administration, a conflict was raging on the proper priority to assign the balance-of-payments problem. On of JFK's advisers, James Tobin, attacked the conventional concern: the domestic restrictions the United States endured for the sake of balance-of-payments rectitude "have not served the world economy well. Neither were they essential. . . . International financial policy is too important to leave to financiers." But Treasury Secretary Dillon cautioned Kennedy against any moves which might upset the foreign central bankers and trigger a raid on the dollar. Dillon, writes Schlesinger, "doubted that we would have the bargaining power to negotiate international monetary reform until we had first strengthened the dollar at home." Kennedy seems to have agreed with Tobin in principle but with Dillon in practice. He wanted to avoid any risk of an international financial crisis—one which the electorate would not understand or even feel, but which would nonetheless embarrass the Democrats. Sensitive to the public's distrust of Keynesian ideology, Kennedy had no wish to pile international unorthodoxy upon domestic.

Thus, the Kennedy Administration never made so explicit a commitment to growth that it was willing to plump for full employment at the cost of serious inflation or chronic dollar drains. When these arguments reappeared in force, growth was once again the victim. "Let me make it absolutely clear," said Treasury Under Secretary Robert Roosa in an adumbration of a subsequent official style, "that there is no thought that foreign exchange operations can provide a solution to the U.S. Balance of Payments deficit. More fundamental correctives are necessary." Almost necessarily, these correctives would include higher U.S. interest rates and slower growth.

A glance at the historical record might suggest that the points of the last paragraph are overdrawn. For a nation uncommitted to growth, the United States did eventually tolerate a great deal of inflation and much embarrassment on the international-payments question rather than cut the expansionary impact of the federal budget. Unemployment never exceeded 4 per cent between late 1965 and late 1968, and output (adjusted for price changes) increased by almost 5 per cent annually. Yet the inflation rate accelerated from about 2 to 5 per cent and the payments deficit increased dramatically.

But this choice of rapid growth over price and foreign exchange stability was not deliberate; it was a by-product of the politics of the Vietnam War. In short, Indochina suspended the usual sacrifice of growth for other objectives because neither the President nor the Congress was willing to acknowledge that even unpopular wars consume resources. The 1964 tax cut brought the economy to full employment in 1965. Hence, by the Keynesian rules of the game, taxes should have been raised or domestic programs cut in order to divert the $30 billion annually needed for arms. But LBJ refused to follow the rules in 1966; he promised both guns and butter. To compound the seriousness of this departure from Keynesian orthodoxy, Vietnam turned out to cost $10 billion more than the Pentagon optimists anticipated. The government was not denied the resources needed to gear up for Vietnam, but in the process the prices of scarce labor and materials began to climb. Steep pay increases in steel and airlines spelled the death of the Kennedy-Johnson "guidelines" for wages and prices. When LBJ finally proposed a 6-percent tax surcharge in response to accelerating prices, Congress refused to accept the responsibility. From the viewpoint of Capitol Hill, it was one thing to provide the President with carte blanche in foreign policy, and quite another to ask constituents to pay for it. If something had to be done, congressmen were fond of observing, somebody should cut out wasteful spending.

Ultimately, in June 1968, Congress raised income taxes by 10 per cent. But the resulting restraint seemed to have little salutary impact. Though output growth slowed down, prices rose at a 5-per-cent clip. Now that the Keynesian remedy for inflation had finally been tried, it seemed not to work. "When we were able to call the policy tune," said Arthur Okun, "the economy did not dance to it."

Two explanations of this apparent failure of the New Economics competed for attention in the first two and a half years of the Nixon Administration. Most economists argued that Keynesian methods were not really discredited by the experience. Prices, they said, did not react as quickly to fiscal policy as did output and employment. Expectations of more inflation were built into union and management thinking by the trauma of 1965–1968. Only a long period of budget restraint—bringing low profits and rising unemployment—would slow down the wage-price spiral.

Another view, which understandably gained popularity as prices stubbornly continued to climb, explained the lag as an example of the futility of fiscal policy. Consumer behavior was too unpredictable to allow "fine-tuning" of the economy through tax and budget changes. A more certain approach to controlling future inflation was to keep a firm grip on the money supply.

This second view, expounded by Milton Friedman and other monetarists, raised the stock of anti-Keynesian economics to its highest level in thirty-five years, but had little direct impact on Nixon's economic policy. The Administration's experts, notably Paul McCracken and Herbert Stein, were Keynesians—less intellectually and emotionally committed than their predecessors, but Keynesians nonetheless. Nixon attempted to beat back the inflation with two years of tight budgets that left nearly 6-per-cent unemployment. The choice of price stability at the cost of jobs was also motivated by the accelerating deterioration of the balance of payments. The dollar outflow reached unprecedented rates in 1970–1971 as currency speculators began to sniff European impatience with American policies. When in 1971 the payments deficit reached an incredible annual rate of $23 billion, it triggered the Administration's New Economic Policy.

With the implementation of wage and price controls on August 15, 1971, the New Economics was formally abandoned. Ironically, Nixon's capitulation came just as prices seemed to be responding to fiscal policy—inflation which had averaged 5.5 per cent in 1970 fell to an annual rate of 4 per cent in the first half of 1971. Even if the Keynesians were not proved wrong by the experience of delayed reaction to fiscal policy, progrowth advocates lost much of the status they had gained from the 1964 tax cut. Nobody had much faith left that the New Economists could fine-tune the economy to sustained economic growth without rapid inflation, and few would be willing to take the risk once more. The danger of a repeat of 1965–1968 could not be logically refuted by the economists who had watched sound anti-inflationary policy recommendations be undermined by the politics of Vietnam. Arthur Okun notes: "Economists were hoping to determine from experience the feasibility of a combination of 4-per-cent unemployment and a 2-per-cent rate of price increase. But the defense spurt ruined that experiment. . . . Vietnam plays the Danish prince in the *Hamlet* of recent economic history."

In the 1950s, rapid growth had been sacrificed to the classic myths of economic orthodoxy—the virtues of unchanging prices, balanced budgets, and international exchange stability. When the long-delayed Keynesian Revolution finally took place, it succeeded in raising the real income of the average American by 15 per cent in just four years. But in the process, the opponents of sustained growth were never vanquished. Success was still measured as much by the avoidance of inflation and exchange deficits as it was by the increase in national income. When price and exchange stability became Vietnam casualties, growth was once more sent to the foot of the table.

Restoration of growth as the major goal of economic policy in the 1970s is going to be tougher than it was in the early 1960s. John Kennedy was able to finesse the opposition with the rhetoric of national purpose—we had to be biggest to be best. Such an argument would be hard to sell in an age when Nixon runs for re-election by visiting Moscow and Peking. The proponents of rapid growth have argued that the technical difficulties of running the economy at capacity were surmountable; now they will be forced also to show that rapid growth is worth its environmental price.

But while the technical opposition to growth now shares the news with the recent concerns about natural-resource scarcity and ecological collapse, its authority still persists. Balance-of-payments and inflation worries remain the most influential constraints on economic policy. It is to these matters that we now turn.

4

The Perils of Inflation

See, we got these books here [base-price books kept in accordance with §300.013 of Title 6 of the Economic Stabilization Act of 1971]. I don't know what it is. Why is that book there? What good is the book? Nobody ever looks at it. Why is the book here? You're a law student, you tell me. . . .

—SUPERMARKET MANAGER, *West 86th Street, New York City*

"Inflation," wrote John Kenneth Galbraith in 1952, "is damaging to the effectiveness and integrity of government and it is destructive of schools, colleges, churches, charitable institutions—in fact of all the amenities which Western man has so laboriously built up and which permit him to describe himself as civilized. It rewards the grossest and most material of talents. No democracy that has experienced a severe or long-continued inflation has survived wholly intact. But inflation is also inimical to production. It rewards equally the man who produces and the man who holds resources out of production for their appreciation in money value. It draws resources from where they are most needed to serve the wants of those who have most profited. So it, also, is inconsistent with maximum useful production."

Conservatives do not like inflation either. Herbert Stein quotes an Eisenhower speech on "the battle for a sound dollar":

> This is not just a fight to balance the budget as an end in itself. This is a fight to keep our nation fiscally strong so that we may maintain the forces we must have for the security of ourselves and the free world. This is a fight to promote an expanding economy and domestic prosperity. This is a fight to make sure that a dollar earned today will tomorrow buy for the housewife an equal amount of groceries.

Inflation, then, is the enemy of national defense, economic expansion, housewives' living standards, colleges, charities, democracies, and maximum useful production. It is, in a familiar orators' phrase, "the cruelest tax of all," cheating old people of their savings and the worker of his wage.

In a while we shall have a word to say about all of these charges. But for the moment it is enough simply to notice that inflation is not very popular. Most people think they are victimized by inflation, and it leads them, rightly or wrongly, to brood about their paycheck and grumble about their President.

The public aversion to inflation has a direct and negative consequence for prosperity and economic growth. High-growth policies are, in practice, full-employment policies. And one of the most dismal observations of modern economics is that there is a trade-off between the rate of inflation and the rate of unemployment. Less of one means more of the other. Hence, full employment (which means an unemployment rate between 3.5 and 4.5 per cent) can, it is estimated, be sustained only with 4- to 5-per-cent inflation. Price stability (a Pickwickian term, meaning annual inflation of no more than 1 to 2 per cent) probably is possible only with more than 5-per-cent unemployment. Put another way, the likely cost of reducing inflation by 1 per cent is the loss of 1 million jobs. As Yale economist William Nordhaus observes, "Inflation is the social cost of low unemployment rates."

Since full employment and inflation are linked together, the public's distaste for inflation has traditionally been translated into a government policy of accepting economic slack. Eisenhower's failure to intervene against recessions in 1954, 1958, and 1960 was justified as essential to avoid runaway inflation. Nixon's deliberate policy of sacrificing high employment was designed to slow down the inflation of the late Johnson years. Thanks to the trade-off between employment and prices, the federal government has never pursued a consistent policy of high growth in peacetime. Nor will it ever, unless the trade-off changes or inflation becomes more palatable.

While economists are reasonably confident of the practical relationship between unemployment and inflation, the mechanics of the process appear quite complex. The basic explanation for the trade-off (known to economists as the "Phillips curve") is that, when business is booming and unemployment is low, labor and management claim wages and profits which together add up to more than the total value of output at current prices. Since not everyone can be satisfied without a rise in prices, inflation becomes a legal and anonymous resolution of these inconsistent and conflicting claims. The size of the economic pie that must be divided doesn't increase, but its value in dollars does. When unemployment and excess productive capacity are high, claims for higher wages and profits are checked by the actual or potential price competition between business firms. Macy's cannot grant a fat pay increase to its workers and pass on the costs to its customers; they'll all shop at Gimbels. But it would take a virtual depression to stabilize prices altogether.

One reason for the inflationary bias of our economy is that strong unions and corporations are insulated against the pressures of competition. When the United Auto Workers asks General Motors for an 8-per-cent wage increase, GM doesn't have to worry very much that it will not be able to pass on the increase to the public; the UAW will be making a similar demand of Ford and of Chrysler. Similarly, the United Auto Workers need not fret that union labor will price itself out of the market and the Big Three will turn to nonunion help; all that was settled decades ago. Over-all, perhaps 14 per cent of the economy is in the hands of business with substantial ability to pass on cost increases; 7 per cent, including housing construction and trucking, is made up of small competitive firms but is dominated by large unions that bargain for wages across the industry; no one firm has to fear that its competitors will have lower labor costs.

Government regulation covers another 6 per cent of GNP (telephone, electric power, gas, trains, buses, airlines); the regulatory agencies customarily turn negotiated wage increases into rate hikes without much second-guessing. Sixteen per cent of the economy represents federal, state, and municipal employment; and an additional 8 per cent involves professions and nonprofit industries (such as health care), which respond loosely, at best, to competitive price pressures. Conservatively, perhaps half the economy falls outside the strict discipline of competition.

Even in the competitive sector of the economy there are powerful forces that push prices up during good times. The crucial factor is the universal reluctance to accept setbacks in money income. Wage rates for a given job can almost never be cut—even at the depths of the recent aerospace-engineering depression, salary reductions for employees were rarely contemplated. When things got bad enough, the company would lay people off or put them on a three-day week but it would never expect anyone to stay on the job at lower pay. Occasionally, a union will vote to accept a pay reduction in order to keep a bankrupt company or hopelessly inefficient plant in business a little longer. When that happens, it is national news; ordinarily, the plant simply disappears.

Many firms, too, would rather lose short-run profits than lower their prices. New York City's taxi fleets, for example, pushed through a 48-per-cent rate hike in March 1971. Soon it developed that business was falling off by perhaps as much as 60 per cent. Cab-owners were making little more money than at the old fares and in some instances less. At some intermediate fare schedule they would probably make a good deal more than at either the cheap old rates or the steep new ones. But few seriously proposed a rollback; it just was not done. (In the case of the regulated cab industry, a rollback might also embarrass the public officials who had granted the original increase and prejudice them against future increase that would be in the owners' interests. But other non-regulated industries may also want to avoid embarrassment in the eyes of their customers or themselves.)

A capitalist economy depends on changes in prices and wages as signals to move labor and other resources from sectors of declining demand to sectors of growing importance.

But if prices and wages can rarely go down, there is only one direction in which they can move in response to changing economic conditions.

Although a slowdown of demand aggravates one disease, unemployment, while ameliorating the other, inflation, the timing of the impact varies. Employment usually dips before inflation levels off. The first reaction of most businesses to disappointing sales is to cut output and employment, not to change their established price lists and wage scales. Meanwhile, the momentum of adjusting prices to past wage increases and wages to past price increases continues. The moderating effects of slack demand on prices and wages occur slowly and indirectly. Thus the Phillips curve does not present an instantaneously obtainable menu of alternatives; the economy cannot be moved from a high level of inflation to a low one by a quick movement along the trade-off curve.

That is why some years, such as 1970, have shown sharp increases in both unemployment and prices. The early-1971 combination of the worst of both worlds—5-per-cent inflation and 6-per-cent unemployment—reflected the difficulty of a transition from several years of rapid price increases. Continuing unemployment at that level would probably have eventually reduced inflation to 1.5 or 2 per cent a year; but the transition might have taken another two years of continued high unemployment.

Recessions aren't good politics, a lesson carefully learned by Vice-President Nixon in 1958, candidate Nixon in 1960, and President Nixon in 1970. Through 1969 and 1970, the Administration patiently tried to manage a gradual and controlled economic slowdown, as the New Economics would prescribe, by restricting the size of the budget deficit and the growth of the money supply. The effects of inflation were disappointing; but in early 1971, the Administration decided that the patient had had enough deflationary medicine even if his symptoms had not disappeared. Nixon vowed to reduce unemployment to 4.5 per cent by campaign time in 1972, by running a large deficit and holding down interest rates. His hope was that we could meanwhile enjoy the best of the two worlds of which we had the worst in 1970. The deflationary medicine of 1970 hit employment and output, but its effects on prices were deferred until 1971–1972. The expansionary medicine of 1971 would, it was hoped, raise employment and output while price inflation was still tapering off.

This 1971 "game plan" was half-successful when the President abandoned it for his August 15 New Economic Policy. Inflation was, indeed, winding down: in the twelve months preceding his August 15 speech, the rate of increase in the Consumer Price Index was only 4.4 per cent, down from 5.9 per cent in the preceding twelve months. Unemployment, however, stubbornly remained at 6 per cent. As predicted by all but the President's Council of Economic Advisers, the Administration's expansionary measures were too weak to make much difference. Nixon, saying "I am a Keynesian," had deliberately embraced deficit spending, sweetening the bitter pill for conservatives by promising to spend no more than the hypothetical revenues the tax system would produce at full employment. But in spite of all the rhetoric about the "full employment" budget, fiscal policy was cautiously slated to be no more expansionary in 1971–1972 than in 1970–1971. Federal expenditures and federal revenues were both, according to budget proposals, to rise at the normal rate of growth of the economy; in each year a "balanced full-employment budget" was projected.

That would not have been enough to restore full employment. And, for additional stimulation by the route of an easy-money policy, the President was dependent on the cooperation of the Federal Reserve Board. However, the Fed's chairman, Arthur Burns, was in no mood to validate the Administration's forecasts and targets. Burns wanted to see more evidence that inflation was abating, and wanted more direct action to control specific wages and prices than the President and his economic advisers, Paul McCracken and Budget Director George Shultz, were willing to take.

By mid-1971, it had become apparent that unemployment would not retreat quickly—or perhaps not at all—without a more expansionary dose of fiscal and monetary policy. The Administration, fearful that expansion would shatter the fragile success of its campaign against inflation, felt itself once more to be trapped by the familiar double-bind of the Phillips curve. Progress toward either of its goals, reduced unemployment or price stability, would mean a setback for the other. Using conventional measures of fiscal and monetary policy, the Administration could either reduce unemployment and risk the acceleration of inflation, or squeeze out inflation at the cost of even worse unemployment. Neither choice had much appeal to a President only sixteen months away from an election. Disenchanted with the unhurried optimism of his customary advisers, Nixon jumped at newcomer John Connally's suggestion that it was time for boldness. The result was the August 15 *coup de théâtre*: the import surcharge, the end to international dollar convertibility, and the wage-price freeze.

Controls were meant to take the place of recession as the means for suppressing inflation. The economy could be allowed to expand, since the inflationary pressure from labor and management would bump up against the legal ceiling. In this way the Administration could at last direct fiscal and monetary policy to easing the problem of unemployment.

But once again the Administration moved in half steps. The President's August speech promised not merely to cut taxes to reduce unemployment, but to reduce federal expenditures by an equivalent amount to fight inflation. If he had really meant what he said, the decline in government spending would have canceled out the stimulation of the tax reduction—and then some. But, in fact, some of the proposed cuts in expenditure were illusory or overstated. Cumulatively, Nixon's budget proposals would create some jobs, but far from enough to restore full employment. Even optimistic estimates predicted a reduction in unemployment from the 6 per cent of July 1971 to only 5.2 per cent by Election Day, 1972.

Nixon's anemic fiscal program was not simply a symptom of a conservative's enduring obsession with balanced budgets. It was, again, a testimony to the perceived hazards of inflation. A full-throttle program of expansion would have severely tested the efficacy of the wage-price controls. Even a sternly enforced system of controls can give way under inflationary pressure. The more rewarding it is to cheat on price controls, the more incentives there are to try. During World War II, black markets flourished in items that were impossible to buy at the legal price. Since the Administration wanted no wage-price bureaucracy and little abrasive enforcement, the problem was even more severe. Low-keyed controls could only succeed in a low-pressure economy. Once more, the Administration was forced to accept high unemployment in order to forestall continued inflation.

The Perils of Inflation 125

A small dose of controls is unlikely to remove the underlying dilemma of the Phillips curve. The restraints against competition built into our economic system have not changed and political realism suggests that they cannot be easily dislodged. The odds are that inflation won't remain in check unless unemployment is kept well above 4 or 4.5 per cent. At best, we will return to the familiar situation of the late 1950s, with unemployment meandering around 5 or 6 per cent because the makers of economic policy are afraid of the inflationary consequences of full employment.

Is that the world we want? Unemployment at 5.5 per cent for the nation translates into between 11 and 12 per cent for the young and for blacks (and perhaps twice that for the black young); it amounts to an annual sacrifice of roughly $55 billion in unproduced output, compared with the full-employment level. In short, victory in the war on inflation has an enormous cost. Perhaps, instead, we should explore the path of peaceful coexistence with inflation, making it more bearable, and learning to live with it.

The first step is understanding just what harm inflation causes. Here, as elsewhere, conventional journalistic and political wisdom is a poor guide. The major charge against inflation is that it redistributes income unfairly. Supposedly, wages lag behind climbing prices and corporate profits. Old people on fixed incomes, savers, welfare recipients, and government employees are all said to suffer a severe loss of purchasing power to the benefit of corporate fat cats.

The facts tell a different story. The major gainers from inflation are not the owners of big business but workers who would have been unemployed or underemployed had prices been kept lower. These workers are, of course, principally the poor, the black, and the young. Last hired and first fired, these groups have the most to gain from a national policy of full employment. In a booming economy, the scarcity of labor coaxes employers to overcome their prejudices and their natural reluctance to hire unskilled labor. Recruiters are dispatched to ghetto schools, most of whose students would in ordinary times be turned away at the door. Married women who have dropped out of the labor force are lured back by higher pay and more flexible jobs. Out-of-work older people find that age is no longer a barrier to employment.

A few statistics suggest the power of full employment to reduce poverty. A 1965 study by Metcalf and Mooney for the Office of Economic Opportunity estimated that a shift from 5.4-per-cent to a 3.5-per-cent national unemployment rate would result in an increase in full-time employment of 1,042,000 for the poor. The net result would be to move 1,811,000 people above the "poverty line" as it is defined by the government.

William Nordhaus has estimated, using 1960 figures, the gains in income consequent on a 1-per-cent reduction in unemployment. For families earning under $2000, the increased employment alone would raise total incomes by over 10 per cent. For those earning between $2000 and $4000, the gain would approximate 2 per cent. At the other end of the scale—for families earning over $10,000—the increase is only one-fiftieth of a per cent. The high employment which can accompany inflation is one of the most strongly egalitarian measures of income redistribution known to the American economy.

Apart from its effect on unemployment, inflation neither systematically helps nor hurts the working man. There is no evidence to suggest that labor's share in the national income

—the percentage of total income paid to workers—deteriorates during periods of inflation. As economists George Bach and Alfred Ando have noted, "During the entire 1939–52 inflation, the labor share rose by 6 per cent of total personal income (from 64 to 70 per cent), contrary to the general notion that wages and salaries lag behind during inflation."

To be sure, in some cases of hyperinflation—accelerating inflation with rates of up to 3000 per cent a month—there is a loss in real wages. The Berlin sales clerk whose pay envelope in November 1923 bulged with 23 trillion Marks was not a prosperous man. Inflation of that magnitude convulsed the German economy and, as Galbraith falsely stated of inflation in general, did indeed reward "the grossest and most material of talents." Money changers and grain hoarders made a fortune; the petty bourgeoisie lost its shirt. But the German money binges have little to do with the 6-per-cent inflation that the United States experienced at the height of Vietnam. Price rises of this magnitude involve no breakdown of normal production or systematic income shift to the rich. Labor's real income is determined, as usual, by productivity and bargaining power, and these are not affected by inflation.

It is true that workers covered by long-term contracts may lose out during the first phase of an inflation. If all prices suddenly went up 4 per cent tomorrow, it would be several months or even a year or two before most workers caught up. But in the course of a continuing inflation the catch-up is complete and fairly continuous. Union contracts are renegotiated to make up for past price increases and anticipate future ones. Even in the unorganized sector of the economy, firms whose products are selling at higher prices find that workers' time is worth more to them, and workers are able to sell their services at higher wages. During the Vietnam inflation of 1965–1969, for example, the after-tax purchasing power of the average wage and salary earner went up by about 17 per cent.

While full employment and the inflation that goes with it do not affect the distribution of income between business and labor, they do alter the relative wages of different kinds of workers; and the gainers in this process are the unskilled and the poorly paid, not the affluent. Full employment creates a shortage of unskilled labor and compresses wage differences.

Tradition has it that Social Security and welfare recipients, as well as workers, suffer economic losses from inflation. Here the charge has had some historical justification. During and immediately after World War II, Social Security payments lagged badly behind the rise in prices. But since the end of the 1940s they have kept up not merely with the inflation, but with the much faster increase in per-capita income. In dollars of constant value (representing purchasing power in terms of 1971 prices), the average monthly pension for a retired worker has increased from $73.68 in 1950 to $132.16 in 1971. Social Security increases have been discontinuous—usually, Congress votes higher benefits a few months before an election—so there can be a lag of one year or so between price increases and compensating changes in benefits. But the biennial adjustment has been reliable; and under new legislation, benefits will be raised automatically with major changes in the cost of living.

Lags have been somewhat more serious for welfare recipients, but, for them as well, benefits have more than kept pace with inflation over the long haul. Again stated in

1971 dollars, General Assistance benefits have gone up from $37.45 a month in 1950 to $64.80 in 1971; while Aid to Dependent Children has increased from $34.79 to $52.30.

While current income—such as wages and welfare receipts —is not much affected by inflation, a rising price level does have a substantial impact on the value of assets. Here a distinction must be made between assets whose value is fixed in money terms (such as bank accounts, bonds, and mortgages) and those which represent other property (homes, stocks, etc.). The latter kind of asset holds its own during inflationary periods—when prices generally are rising, so does the price of a house and the earnings potential of a business. If the dollar is worth 4 per cent less, the physical assets of General Motors are probably worth 4 per cent more—and so is its stock. The linkage is never exact, but on balance it is neither homeowners nor stockholders who suffer from rising prices.

Inflation does, however, shrink the worth of most assets with a specific money value. For example, interest rates on bonds and mortgages go up along with prices. This means that the currently outstanding obligations, paying lower rates of interest, are actually worth less to their owners than they were before.

Inflation, then, brings capital depreciation for bondholders and other long-term lenders, and a gain for corporate borrowers and the owners of mortgaged homes. Wealth is redistributed from creditors to debtors. But the point to notice is that creditors are generally the more prosperous group, and the redistribution accomplished by inflation is a progressive one. Bonds are no encumbrance for the poor, and mortgage payments flow from average-income homeowners to the far wealthier proprietors of banks.

To be sure, inflation is harsh on one group of modest means—small savers with accounts in banks or savings and loan associations. But here the blame lies not with inflation itself, but rather with a series of government regulations that clamp a maximum limit on the interest rates that banks and savings and loans can pay. Without the ceiling, savings-account rates would keep pace with the over-all rise in interest rates during inflationary times. Savers would earn more on their dollar, canceling out the decline in each dollar's value.

As it happens, though, this kind of automatic protection against inflation is available only to wealthy investors. A man with $25,000 to salt away in late 1969 could have chosen "commercial paper" (short-term bonds sold by large corporations like GM and Sears) paying a comfortable 8 per cent. But with $3000 in savings, he could only have gone to the bank (or bought low-interest U.S. savings bonds); commercial paper isn't sold in small lots. The bank, in turn, would pay him at the government-set maximum of 4 per cent for savings deposits—or less than his annual loss from the 6-per-cent rate of inflation.

Over-all, our only major concern about the effect of inflation on the distribution of income should be for pensioners and small savers, and it would be much less painful to subsidize pensions and remove discriminatory interest ceilings than to suppress inflation.

A more fundamental problem is raised by Milton Friedman and other economists who deny that we can reap the gains of high employment by choosing to live with more inflation. They argue that there is no long-run trade-off between inflation and unemployment. The Phillips curve, in their view, expresses only short-run alternatives. In the long run, there is only one "natural" rate of unemployment for a country's economy. If we try to reduce unemployment beyond this point we may have some temporary success, but the resulting price increases will prod unions and other workers to raise their wage demands and induce employers to grant them. Once again, the sum of wage and profit claims will exceed the value of output available to satisfy them. An even higher rate of inflation will be necessary to resolve this conflict.

Moreover, Friedman argues, this new round of inflation will also, in turn, be reflected in a new round of wage demands. As a result, the Phillips curve trade-off will become worse. Where initially we might have been able to choose 3-per-cent inflation, we might soon have to accept 6-per-cent inflation for the same rate of joblessness. Over time, in this view, the economy cannot choose its rate of unemployment, but can merely decide how much inflation it wishes to endure in a futile attempt to alter that rate.

Friedman's argument claims to rest on the assumption that you can't fool all of the people all of the time. If labor and business are together demanding returns totaling more than output, then, in Friedman's view, a mere reshuffling of prices and wages through inflation will not resolve the conflict. But, in fact, the evidence suggests that even sophisticated people are far more sensitive to direct losses in money incomes than to declines in their purchasing power through higher prices. Wage and salary reductions are almost unknown in industrial countries, even though it is not uncommon for employees to suffer temporary losses in purchasing power. So long as wages and prices are set in dollars, and money retains its age-old power to deceive, inflation can be used to resolve economic conflict.

Statistical studies have yet to verify a one-for-one feedback of price rises on to subsequent wage demands; current estimates for the United States are that from 35 per cent to 70 per cent of price increases are ultimately translated into subsequent wage increases. This does not mean that labor is losing out—prices do not for long move more than in proportion to wage costs—but simply that there is a damper on the inflationary process. Ultimately, inflation may be no more deceptive than the change of the monetary unit from, for example, old francs to new francs with two fewer zeros, and have no greater effect on real behavior. Perhaps "money illusion" is a transient phenomenon. But the period of adjustment is better measured in decades than in years. If so, the Phillips trade-off is real enough for the practitioners of economic policy.

Everyone can agree to one implication of the feedback of price inflation to future wages and prices: the alternatives we face are more unfavorable than first appears. Thus, the full cost in inflation of the high-employment policy as of 1966 and 1968 will be far more substantial than what was immediately felt. But observe that anticipated inflation is harmless inflation. The same foresight that gives it momentum means that few are caught unaware by the "cruelest tax." And if the sting is gone from inflation, there is little wrong with having more of it.

Removing the sting has not been seriously considered as an alternative to anti-inflationary policy. Yet it is not hard to devise measures that would make inflation less painful and inequitable. People living on low, fixed private pensions could be granted federal cost-of-living supplements, just as those who suffer unemployment as a result of government policy are given public assistance. The discriminatory ceiling on bank and savings-and-loan deposit rates could be removed. Cost-of-living escalators could be built into welfare and Social Security payments, and both small savers and pension funds could be offered an inflation-proof bond with adjustable interest payments. There is no reason why a nation with a financial structure as elaborate and costly as ours cannot find a way to allow ordinary people to protect themselves against inflation.

These measures may seem to be palliatives, with the drawback of delaying a more fundamental solution. Inflation can abate only when one or another group in society is forced to settle for less real income than it had previously been striving to obtain. If old people and welfare recipients are protected, some other group—more affluent and perhaps politically more powerful—must make the sacrifice. Cost-of-living protection may make the economy somewhat more prone to inflation, while distributing the burden of inflation far more fairly. Still the bargain seems attractive, since any remaining harm from inflation must be weighed against the gains in employment and output. So long as a more fundamental solution means chronic high unemployment, we are not in a position to be scornful of palliatives.

Conventionally, one reservation would have to be imposed in this case for cushioned inflation. Concern for the balance of payments should, the argument goes, limit our freedom to inflate at will. As long as the exchange rate between the dollar and other currencies is kept fixed, inflation in the United States that is faster than that in the rest of the world will eventually retard our exports, increase our imports, and push more dollars into the hands of nervous foreign governments and central bankers. Again, we may face the prospect of a "run on the dollar" such as the one which prompted

President Nixon's economic about-face of August 1971. But the answer to these problems, as we argue in the next chapter, is to try to break the link between domestic policy and balance-of-payments repercussions.

In sum, it makes sense to aim at the 4-per-cent unemployment rate, which would in effect mean full employment, and work to moderate the effects of the inflation that comes with it. But it is also worthwhile to take whatever measures we can to diminish, over the long run, the inflationary bias of the economy.

Improving labor mobility is the least controversial prescription. Anything that helps to match unemployed workers with unfilled jobs—computerized placement, retraining, moving allowances—helps to reduce unemployment without accelerating inflation. Some programs exist already, but much more can be done.

Reduction of monopoly power is a more important, and less tractable, task. One reason for the Phillips dilemma is that strategically placed unions and industries can claim more in income than they produce, with little discipline from competition. For example, when they face high and rising demand, they can be quick to raise wages and prices. When they confront falling demand, their wages and prices do not respond. A thorough solution would require curbing these concentrations of economic power.

But this sort of reform is not easy; nor is it unequivocally desirable. Curbing the monopolistic wage-setting power of unions, for example, would inevitably weaken their ability to seek nonwage objectives. A castrated steelworkers' union which could not affect wage rates would also, in all probability, have little to say about work safety or the conduct of grievance proceedings. Nor would it have much influence on

Congress or state legislatures. To libertarians who can seriously imagine an America devoid of concentrated power, this would be all to the good. But to realistic liberals the stakes are more serious. Those who have written off the union movement as a preserve of self-seeking middle-Americanism would do well to imagine another organized constituency for income-redistribution or full-employment policies, or another source of political opposition to corporate self-seeking. One could, of course, aim the weapon of reform only at the most monopolistic of unions, which are simultaneously the most conservative: the guilds in construction and the other skilled trades. Here the problem is simply political: if Congress ever did pass another round of antiunion legislation it would predictably be directed, like the Taft-Hartley Act, at the weakest unions.

Another possibility is stricter antitrust action in industries dominated by a few firms. Much of America's manufacturing is conducted by oligopolists—firms that share a market with a few giant rivals: the Big Three in autos, three in aluminum (Kaiser, Reynolds, Alcoa), two in aircraft engines (GE, Pratt-Whitney). Antitrust enforcers have generally kept their distance from these great concentrations of power. To be sure, direct collusion among competitors is a criminal offense, occasionally detected. Far more common is a pattern of habitual coincidence of action: Consolidated raises its prices, so Amalgamated follows suit, without any clandestine meetings or coded conversations. Briefly, in the late 1930s, the Justice Department's Antitrust Division began an attack on "price leadership" and tacit collusion in concentrated industries. The Supreme Court seemed willing to go along. But World War II intervened, corporate America went to war, and antitrust was put out to pasture. Only very recently, in a Federal Trade Commission action against the Big Four cereal manufacturers, has any federal enforcement agency pursued the theory that these dominant firms in concentrated markets constitute "shared monopolies" and are vulnerable to antitrust attack. A revival of public preoccupation with corporate power, sparked by Ralph Nader and the "New Populists," may put some muscle behind the commission's attack. Legislation to break up major oligopolies was proposed by President Johnson's antitrust task force and seconded in early 1972 by the major Democratic candidates.

But even if this new antitrust offensive survives the inevitable obstacle course in the bureaucracy and the courts, there will remain the problem of fashioning a remedy. Suppose that the largest manufacturing firms are indeed illegal participants in "shared monopolies": should they be dissolved? Would we be better off with General Motors split into eight parts, General Foods diced into six? Perhaps, but it is still a matter of conjecture. Conceivably, half-billion-dollar giant corporations are more innovative or efficient than $97-million weaklings; and if they are, society might be better off forgiving them their possession and exercise of some monopoly power. Evidence on this question is meager, but what there is suggests that gigantic firms are *not* systematically better innovators than those of smaller size. Indeed, a disproportionate share of the major technological innovations of the century have come from small firms or lone inventors, such as xerography's Chester Carlson and television's Philo T. Farnsworth. Thus, we may risk little by breaking big companies into smaller units. But the process is cumbersome and the gains uncertain. We would be unwise to count on antitrust as a panacea for inflation.

Even if domestic monopolies and oligopolies are not dismembered, their power can often be controlled by permitting unrestricted foreign competition. GM, when it wants to raise its car prices, now has to worry about its competitors in Göteborg and Stuttgart as well as its friendly rivals in Detroit. The sluggish, chummy steel companies have had their habits of price leadership and technological backwardness shaken by stiff competition from abroad. What the American antitrust laws won't do, free trade often can.

But, again, the problem is political. For years, powerful industries have been able to exempt themselves from a national commitment to free trade. Oil import quotas keep out cheap foreign petroleum at a cost to consumers of over $5 billion a year. Quotas on food imports prop up the price-support system and help fatten the business farmer. Now, to these long-standing trade barriers a new obstacle course may be added, thanks to public distaste for Asian competition. Japanese television sets and steel bars, Taiwanese cotton textiles, and Korean synthetics have all had their impact on American politics. "I am not really for having a trade war," conceded Xerox President C. Peter McColough in a statement typical even of the export-minded side of American business, "but until the government, or the President, or somebody else has the power to strike back quickly and hard, we will not get anywhere with Japan." Companies threatened by import competition have been even more blunt. "We've only seen the beginning," said Henry Ford II, speaking of the displacement of Mustangs and Pintos by Toyota Coronas in the West Coast market. "Wait until those Japs get ahold of the central part of the United States." The American labor movement, briefly converted to free trade during the 1950s and 1960s, has joined the protectionist united front. Labor-supported legislation would place quota restrictions on practically all American imports. American firms would be forbidden to invest money abroad, or license their patents for foreign use, if the President decided there were a threat to American jobs. This new protectionist program would, in the words of *New York Times* economist Leonard Silk, "make the Smoot-Hawley Tariff of 1930 look as if it might have been written by Adam Smith."

These rumblings from threatened industrialists and displaced workers have forced Congress and the President to hedge their commitments to freer trade. Under pressure from Congress, the Nixon Administration pressed Japan to agree on "voluntary" export quotas for textiles, steel, and electronics, sharply inhibiting her growth of exports in years to come. The near-term prospect is, at best, for a standstill on tariffs and quotas and no significant further reduction through trade of domestic monopoly power.

A more promising possibility is reform of the regulatory agencies: the Interstate Commerce Commission, the Civil Aeronautics Board, the Federal Power Commission, and the like. These brave alphabet agencies of the Progressive and New Deal eras are finally being recognized by liberals for the failures they have long since become. Many of the regulatory agencies did not have to "sell out"—they were designed from the outset to strangle competition and succor monopoly. The Interstate Commerce Commission, we now know, was welcomed by many of the railroads as a means of halting rate wars.* American Telephone and Telegraph

---

* Those railroads which had been initially suspicious were quickly reassured. The classic text is a letter from President Cleveland's Attorney-General-designate, Richard Olney, to the president of a railroad who had asked him to help abolish the ICC. "My impression," wrote Olney, "would be that, looking at the matter from a railroad point of view exclusively, [abolition of the ICC] would not be a wise thing to undertake. . . . The attempt would

begged for government regulation when its patents expired and rivals started stringing up telephone lines. The Civil Aeronautics Board has always been a device for fixing prices, splitting markets, and fencing out competitors, keeping the cost of airline tickets up to 40 per cent higher than necessary.

As the agencies matured, so did their obligations to corporate power. The ICC, once run by the railroads, modernized by selling out to the truckers. It is now in the business of keeping truck rates high by excluding new firms, and keeping railroad rates even higher to prevent them from competing. As a sideline, the ICC publishes a tough truck-safety code, which it does not enforce, and a weak household-movers' code, which it also does not enforce.

Today this form of sweetheart regulation has accumulated a diverse coalition of enemies. Conservative economists of the "Chicago school" are being joined in their critique of regulation by Nader's Raiders and the decentralist left. But the old liberal enthusiasm for pervasive regulation of business "in the public interest" does not die an easy death. Generations of liberal lawyers have gone to work for the alphabet agencies or for the Washington law firms that insure their futility (or for both, in that order). The more perceptive recognize that business regulates the agencies, not vice

---

not be likely to succeed; if it did not succeed, and were made on the ground of the inefficiency and uselessness of the Commission, the result would very probably be giving it the power it now lacks. The Commission, as its functions have now been limited by the courts, is, or can be made, of great use to the railroads. It satisfies the popular clamor for a government supervision of railroads, at the same time that the supervision is almost entirely nominal. Furthermore, the older such a Commission gets to be, the more inclined it will be to take the business and railroad view of things. It becomes a sort of barrier between the railroad corporations and the people and a sort of protection against hasty and crude legislation hostile to railroad interests. . . . The part of wisdom is not to destroy the Commission, but to utilize it."

versa. But most of the young advocates who came to work for the regulatory agencies have become old apparatchiks, wedded to the institutions they sometimes criticize. Few are willing to consider such radical remedies as abolishing regulation and encouraging competition. It is more comforting to believe that the Interstate Commerce Commission and the Civil Aeronautics Board will someday rise from the dead, incorruptible.

Apart from ideology, Democratic as well as Republican legislators have had their own reasons for going soft on the regulatory-industrial complex. The regulated industries have the knack for making and keeping friends: AT&T forgets about campaign bills; California savings-and-loan executives bankroll the Democratic machine; newspaper editors smile back at the supporters of the Failing Newspaper Act (which softens antitrust legislation for the benefit of publishers). Few politicians have been completely immune.

State and local regulation is even more cozily political than the Washington brand. State public-utilities commissions are typically understaffed, underfinanced, and under the thumb of their client industries. State regulation of insurance rates was called into being specifically to ward off federal control; it freely permits (and sometimes enforces) cartel pricing. Resale-price-maintenance laws in many states permit manufacturers and high-priced retailers to exclude competition from discount stores. Professional licensing boards are straightforward devices for limiting access to the profession and propping up fees. Taxi-medallion systems, like New York City's, keep rates high and insure monopoly profits.

These obstacles notwithstanding, the current antiregulatory movement will probably achieve some success. The

Nixon Administration, making a rare choice for free-market ideology over business self-interest, proposed in 1972 a partial deregulation of ground transportation. The international air cartel, buoyed by government regulation here and abroad, has had its wings clipped by the charter-flight entrepreneurs and their $190 round-trip transatlantic fares. If international rates plummet, domestic fares may eventually follow suit. But Congress's instinctive reaction to the news of lower Atlantic fares was to thrust new powers on the CAB, allowing the board to retaliate against foreign airlines that have the audacity to lower prices. The prospect is perhaps for some erosion of the worst types of regulation, but not far enough or fast enough significantly to impede inflation.

While parts of the old, industrial sector of the economy may be freed from government regulation, no such prospect is in store for the newer service sectors. Government financing of health and higher education will inevitably increase; and with public funds come higher prices. The health industry has shown this linkage at its most extreme. In 1964, Congress passed Medicare and Medicaid; from 1964 to 1969, health prices went up 37 per cent, double the over-all cost-of-living increase, while hospital daily service charges soared by an astonishing 77 per cent. The problem was not that the government was throwing its money around, but that the nation's medical system automatically turns an increase in demand for its services into a brisk escalation of costs.

The health industry is inflation-prone largely because those who make the decisions about medical care aren't the ones who foot the bills: 60 per cent of all medical bills are now being paid by private insurers or the government—up from 35 per cent in 1950—and the result is that neither the patients (who don't have to pay) nor doctors and hospitals (who get the money) have any reason to keep costs down.

Health insurers might be expected to police against waste and hospital overuse, but they don't. It is safer to pay for what the doctor ordered than to risk charges of "third-party interference" with medical care. And, more culpably, the insurers see their role as the hospital's collection agent rather than its prudent customer. Blue Cross, private insurance companies, and federal Medicare and Medicaid administrations pay hospitals on a cost-pass-through basis. This device keeps hospitals about as efficient as the average missile contractor. "There are few checks on hospital administrators who purchase prestige by investing other people's money in fancy new equipment," writes lawyer and health planner John Daum; "in one year, 240 of 776 hospitals whose managements had equipped them with open-heart surgery facilities had no cases at all."

One proposed answer to this malfeasance is simple: abolish the private health-insurance industry and substitute comprehensive national health insurance. The Kennedy-Griffiths health-insurance bill, devised by liberal medics and union leaders convoked by the late Walter Reuther, would make most health services available to everyone for free. Doctors would receive federal paychecks, and the AMA nightmare of "socialized medicine" would be here at last.

But socialized medicine à la Kennedy-Griffiths might not resemble its British, Russian, or Israeli models; nor would it automatically reverse the escalation in health costs. So far, the federal government has shown little more ability than health insurers to squeeze the profiteering and waste out of medicine. National health insurance may make decent health care more available, but it is unlikely to make it less costly.

The chances are overwhelming that structural reforms to increase mobility and competition will happen slowly, if at all. In the meantime, if we want to improve the inflation-unemployment trade-off we must consider a more direct approach. The alternatives are public job creation, guideposts (what Paul Samuelson has called "talking the Phillips curve down"), and controls.

Public-service employment is a logical, direct solution to the paradox of a weak economy: that men are idle while urgent tasks abound. Give men shovels, and they can build nature trails; give them mortar, and they can make libraries. But, in the past, job-creating programs have been beset by difficulty. We have expected too much of them: their jobs must go to the hard-core unemployed (lest the programs simply compete with private businesses for the services of the skilled); they must offer a real chance for training and advancement; and they must give people useful work, not simply dig-and-fill assignments.

In theory, all of these objectives could be met. In practice, they are at war with each other. A project manager who is rewarded for getting the job done on time, or improving his workers' skills, will try to hire the most adaptable employees rather than the most unemployable. The more closely he is held to all three objectives, the more the program will cost. Experiments continue, results may improve, and some kind of job-creating program will probably be part of any sensible full-employment policy. But, again, the results to be expected are modest.

"Guideposts" were an effort by the Kennedy and Johnson Administrations to reduce the inflation to be expected from a fully employed economy. Major wage and price decisions were to be guided by principles of noninflationary behavior. Wages, according to the guideposts, should rise by no more than the annual increase in labor productivity in the economy as a whole. In order to keep the over-all price index steady, prices should fall in industries with above-average productivity gains, and rise in laggard sectors.

Some economists, particularly Chicago economists, bluntly dismiss guideposts as so much empty talk, futile "jawboning." Their case is simply that businessmen and unions pursue their self-interests, not some complicated algebraic formulation of the common good. Even if the spirit of cooperation could be counted on for initial compliance with the guideposts, the swift multiplication of exceptions, ambiguities, and outright violations would soon undermine the program. Even if most executives and union leaders want to be good citizens, no one wants to be a sucker.

The evidence on the effects of guideposts is somewhat less pessimistic. Guideposts under favorable circumstances may, it seems, possibly reduce the level of inflation to be expected from any given rate of unemployment. The reduction is not large—one half of 1 per cent is a generous estimate—but it is better than nothing. During the early 1960s guideposts seemed to have this effect. Why they worked is unclear. The Kennedy steel-price confrontation may have made big business wary of government retaliation if prices rose too sharply. Alternatively, guideposts might simply have helped to deflate price and wage expectations. Since inflation often proceeds through futile attempts to stay ahead of the race, one way of curbing today's inflation is to convince everyone

The Perils of Inflation 145

that tomorrow's won't be so bad.

To have this result, guideposts must be within shooting distance of the wages and prices that business and labor are already counting on. Thus, after a year of 5-per-cent inflation, it is hopeless to ask workers to settle for a 3.2-per-cent annual wage increase (the Kennedy Administration's target figure). Some adjustment must be made for the previous loss of purchasing power. Unrealistic limits helped to torpedo the guideposts during the first years of the Vietnam inflation.

President Nixon began his Administration by renouncing the use of guideposts and other "jawboning" techniques. Big business followed suit with a series of price increases which seem to have been postponed until right after the Inauguration. By one estimate, wholesale-price inflation ran .5 per cent higher in 1969 than economic conditions might explain. Over-all, the Administration's shift from jawbone to wishbone did not bring better luck, and its bouts in early 1971 with the steel corporations and construction unions indicated a slight change of strategy. But the main line of the Administration was against guideposts and controls until the very eve of the New Economic Policy.

When the controls did come, they more closely resembled the over-all freeze of prices and wages adopted during the Korean War than they did the detailed OPA price schedules in effect during World War II. A case can be made that the Korean controls were useful in bringing a rapid inflation to a fairly smooth halt. Controls were imposed just as the brisk rise in prices caused by the beginning of the war was leveling off; thus the ceilings were superfluous in many areas of the economy, while elsewhere their mere existence helped to brake inflationary expectations. The prices of raw materials, in particular, were sensitive to expectations of future price changes and had been crucial contributors to the inflationary spiral. Before controls were adopted, speculation had pushed wholesale prices ahead by 15 per cent in six months. The price freeze helped to reverse this trend and prevent it from spreading to the rest of the economy.

The economic situation of mid-1971 was strikingly similar to that at the outset of Korean controls. Once more, inflation coexisted with a soft economy; as mentioned, the rate of inflation had already decreased to 4.4 per cent (in the twelve months preceding the imposition of controls) from 5.9 per cent in the previous year. Unemployment, at 6 per cent, attested to the existence of slack throughout the economy. As in 1952, sluggish consumer demand was a powerful inducement for businessmen to comply with the ceilings.

To be sure, controls probably had some independent effect of their own. The total price increase for the first nine months of controls was 2.1 per cent, down from 3 per cent in the preceding nine months. Some part of this reduction probably would have taken place without controls, but the controls themselves cut the annual rate of inflation by perhaps one-half or 1 percent.

If the Phase II controls worked at all, it was not because of any threat of their enforcement. From the outset, Phase II was an exercise in formalized jawboning, backed up by the majesty of the law but not really by its muscle. The Phase II rules for wages and salaries were so confusing, administration so inept, and violations so common and notorious, that no businessman had much to fear from any violation not shouted from the rooftops.

Administration of price controls was somewhat less arbitrary and chaotic, but here, too, there was ample room for evasion. As the chief of investigations and compliance for an Internal Revenue Service district said, "We are not consciously looking for prosecutions." Rather than use the term "violations" when talking with misbehaving businessmen, "we say instead, 'you are not in compliance.' "

Whatever effect the controls have had has been, in a sense, voluntary. Most people are reluctant explicitly to break the law; and if they are not, their accountants and lawyers are. Experienced labor mediators suggest that the wage controls, confused as they have been, held down wage settlements in early 1972 by perhaps 1 or 2 per cent. Doubtless this has had its impact on prices.

Are permanent controls, then, the answer to inflation? Permanent controls are bound to be detailed controls, demanding a far larger bureaucracy and far stiffer enforcement than the good-natured efforts of Phase II. The more detailed controls become, and the longer they last, the more obvious their inequities will appear. The economy's wage structure is not based on logic or fairness, but rather on supply, demand, and bargaining power. There are no agreed standards for a government board to use in determining which workers or businesses "ought" to receive increases. Should machinists get 5 per cent more while typists are limited to 2 per cent— or vice versa? Should Monsanto be allowed a 3-per-cent increase on sulfuric acid, while Dow Chemical must hold the line on dichlorodifluoro-ethylene? During World War II, with the entire economy controlled, the public accepted a certain amount of arbitrariness in wage and price decisions —though it also countenanced chiseling, evasion, and a vast black market. The mood of the post-Vietnam 1970s would seem to be less congenial. Permanent controls covering the whole economy in peacetime are still politically unthinkable.

Somewhat more plausibly, we might retain controls for the largest firms and unions, hoping to counter their monopoly power with government regulation. But even this solution could well prove politically treacherous. If we are not willing to have the government set one wage for all the lathe operators in the country, would we accept one federally set rate for those at GM and another for those at Lockheed? The unions regard the autonomy of collective bargaining as an indivisible principle, and on practical grounds they may be right.

Apart from politics, the record of the government agencies which regulate monopolies does not inspire enthusiasm for direct regulation of nonmonopoly giants as well. In all likelihood the new agency would sell out, flunk out, or both, becoming in short order a mechanism for suppressing competition or promoting the arbitrary enthusiasms of the regulators.

One alternative, first suggested by Leonard Chazen, would be to give the wage and price board authority only over those industries and unions receiving special government protection from competition—through subsidies, tariffs, quotas, tax preferences, or other kinds of favoritism. The oil industry would not be prohibited from raising its prices so long as foreign supplies were kept off the market. If steel asked for import protection the quid pro quota would be government supervision. Unions benefiting from the Davis-Bacon Act (requiring that government contractors pay union-scale wages even if these are out of line with the prevailing wage in the community) would have a bureaucrat

The Perils of Inflation   *149*

looking over their shoulders at contract time. The idea is appealing but probably presupposes a degree of political opposition to subsidies that, if it existed, could defeat the subsidies directly.

When all these remedies are weighed and pondered, the unpleasant fact remains that full employment implies creeping inflation. We had better recognize that the costs of such inflation are much less than the costs of avoiding it. A sensible policy would pursue full employment and act to cushion the inflation that results. Automatic pension and welfare adjustments and an end to discrimination against small savers could virtually eliminate any hardship from this course of action.

Unlimited or quickly accelerating inflation is not the answer. Apart from its doubtful efficacy in reducing unemployment below a certain minimum level, there is a more pressing objection to accelerating inflation. People think they are being hurt—even if they are not. The brisk, unexpected increases in the price level during the late 1960s made millions of Americans—even those who enjoyed substantial gains in real purchasing power—vastly more anxious about their economic condition. If their anxiety was largely unfounded, it was nonetheless real. Sane economic policy must attempt to educate the public to its actual economic interests; but it must also adapt to persisting fears and apprehensions.

But the result need not be the stop-go policies of the Eisenhower and Nixon Administrations, or the go-slow caution of the first Kennedy years. A steady, growing economy with lower-than-Vietnam inflation would be far less disturbing to most Americans than the fits and starts of recent years. Nobody likes to pay twenty cents for a cup of coffee, but almost everyone is better off than when coffee cost a nickel.

5

The Balance of Payments:
The Cross of Gold

There are few vestiges left of that charming pre-1914 world.
. . . The Viennese waltz is gone in favor of the cha-cha; stately
Edwardian coaches have been replaced by compact hot-rods;
peaceful international relations are but a memory or a dream.
But the fraternity of central bankers bravely carries on under
heavy odds. The Kings of Europe used to address each other in
their letters as "Dear Brother." One almost suspects that the
central bank governors addressed each other as "Dear Cousin."
—PAUL A. SAMUELSON (1961)

President John F. Kennedy, wrote Arthur Schlesinger, Jr.,
"used to tell his advisers that the two things which scared
him the most were nuclear war and the payments deficit. He
had acquired somewhere, perhaps from his father, the belief
that a nation was only as strong as the value of its currency;
and he feared that, if he pushed things too far, 'loss of confidence' would descend and there would be a run on gold."

Eisenhower's fears were at least as vivid. In 1959 he was asked to explain why he would not act to reverse the deepening recession:

Well, remember, balancing the budget is not of interest merely to ourselves. Our friends, the nations with whom we trade, the nations that are increasingly using the dollar as a medium of exchange, they are interested in the knowledge that we can meet our bills.

In fact, America could not and did not pay her bills during the 1960s. From a position in the first postwar decade of chronic balance-of-payments surplus—that is, of payments to the United States from our exports and investments exceeding the amount we owed to foreigners—the United States moved into deeper and deeper deficit. Cumulatively, from 1960 to 1970 we incurred a total deficit of $35 billion. Some of this we paid in gold. But, at its height, our gold hoard was never above $25 billion. By July 1971, our gold and international reserves amounted only to $13 billion, while our balance-of-payments deficit was mounting at the incredible rate of $23 billion a year. Something, it seemed, would have to give.

Something did. Without even a show of consultation with foreign governments, President Nixon announced a New Economic Policy, unilaterally altering the rules of world finance. Fearing the same run on the bank that had terrorized Eisenhower and Kennedy, Nixon proclaimed that dollars held abroad by other nations could no longer be converted into gold. Under the international monetary system, which had prevailed from 1946 until Nixon's speech, the value of all foreign currencies was, in practice, set in dollars, and the value of the dollar was set in gold. With the dollar no longer convertible into gold, its value in foreign currencies was allowed to fluctuate on the world exchange markets. Rapidly it declined.

Thus Nixon put an end to the system of fixed international exchange rates. Simultaneously he imposed a 10-percent surcharge on imports, in violation of the General Agreement on Tariffs and Trade. And he denounced the "unfair edge" possessed by America's foreign competitors and pledged that the United States would no longer compete "with one hand tied behind her back." Suddenly, one Sunday, we were at war with Japan.

A few months later an uneasy peace was restored. Nixon had achieved most of his objectives: a hefty devaluation of American currency, a continued suspension of the convertibility of the dollar into gold, and a commitment from the world's major economic powers to at least discuss U.S. trade grievances. With the devaluation making Swiss chocolate and French champagne more expensive in the United States, and IBMs and Arizona soybeans cheaper in foreign lands, the U.S. could expect a strong improvement in its trade position and, perhaps, an end to its payments deficits. For the time being, American economic policy might proceed without immediate fear "that we cannot meet our bills."

But one thing did not change in these months of hectic negotiation: the continuing assumption that balance-of-payments deficits are worthy of paramount concern and deserve precedence over domestic prosperity and growth. As thoroughly as had Eisenhower and Kennedy, Nixon bought the notion that America's massive deficits were a source of national weakness, a cause for blunt confrontations with foreigners and furrowed introspection at home. "Can we compete any more? Have Americans gone soft?" Nixon asked a panel of experts briefing him on trade policy in the fall of 1971. With American imports exceeding exports for the first time since 1898, the question seemed long overdue.

But America's balance-of-payments position is far less important than politicians and many economists have thought, and utterly unworthy of the sacrifices of well-being that have been made in its name. International trade is a minor business for the United States. It accounts for only 5 per cent of GNP. If a "trade war" broke out tomorrow between the United States, Japan, and the Common Market, most Americans would barely feel the difference. Rents would stay the same; food prices would only be slightly altered, since restrictive trade policies already in force limit U.S. imports. Dubonnet and Yamahas would become more expensive. But for the vast majority of consumers who drink beer and drive Chevys, things would be pretty much the same.

For some businessmen and laborers, however, the change would be more dramatic. More Boeing workers would be out of jobs if foreigners stopped buying 747s, while Detroit might perk up if Volkswagens were driven from the American market. Foreign countries, too, would know that something was happening: exports make up 15 per cent of the Japanese economy, 25 per cent of Germany's, 30 per cent of Great Britain's. Hence Nixon's 10-per-cent import surcharge (imposed on August 15, 1971, and lifted after the currency settlement in November of the same year) shook up the Japanese stock market and sent tremors through the *bourses* of Europe, but its over-all effect on the American economy was minimal.

The reality of self-sufficiency makes trade more a question of politics than of economics for Americans. That, of course, does not mean that trade is insignificant. In domestic politics the minority of workers and corporations whose fortunes hinge on trade often counts for more than the general run of consumers. The big auto manufacturers, in particular, have been hit hard by foreign competition; so have the makers of steel and television sets. These corporations, and their workers' unions, are listened to when hurt. The remarkable increase in American imports during the late 1960s—23 per cent between 1967 and 1968 alone—gored some highly placed oxen. "Tens of thousands of American workers are suffering loss of jobs," said AFL-CIO President George Meany. "It is the government's trade and investment policies that have been responsible in the most part for this situation." With British stereo equipment vying for a leading position in U.S. markets, Japanese color-television sets outshining their domestic competitors, and Belgian steel bars cascading into East Coast ports, political pressure at home has been building up for a major overhaul of America's generally free-trade policies. "The days are past," says U.S. Steel Chairman Edwin Gott, "when this country can afford the kind of 'Marshall Plan' thinking which caters to foreign economies at the expense of our own." (Of course, allowing cheap Belgian steel into the United States caters to the American consumer at least as much as it does to the Belgian producer, but, rhetorically, free trade has been besmirched as a species of altruism.)

Internationally, the fact that the United States is not dependent on trade gives her freedom to use economic policy as a tool for her political objectives—she can spend money abroad to stage wars, shore up allies, or build up national prestige, without worrying too much about the effect on domestic jobs and output. The economic insignificance of American trade underlines the perversity of the government's balance-of-payments obsession. Perhaps the best illustration is Nixon's 1971 New Economic Policy. Its chief results—suspension of the convertibility of the dollar, realignment of exchange rates, and pressure for institutional reform of world finance—may be salutary in the long run. But the announced motivation of the New Economic Policy could hardly have been more perverse. Advertised as an act of national self-assertion, the program's logic had nothing to do with the economic self-interest of the United States. It derived instead from three quite different impulses: pure protectionism, designed to keep foreigners from competing with domestic industries; neomercantilism, a modern version of the sixteenth-century notion that a country's strength is measured not by its productive power but by its hoard of precious metals and foreign currencies; and a curious kind of banker's morality, which regards balance-of-payments deficits as a form of mortal sin.

The protectionist aspect is perverse but understandable. A devaluation of the dollar *lowers* the real wealth and income of the United States and *raises* that of other countries. We have to pay the Japanese more dollars for each Honda, while the Japanese pay us fewer yen for every drill press. For that reason it seems curious that the United States should have to—or want to—bully Europe and Japan into accepting an American devaluation. But while the over-all wealth of a country is virtually certain to diminish with devaluation, the position of its exporters, and of domestic producers who compete with imports, improves.

American exporters are helped by devaluation because their products can be sold at a lower price in foreign markets without any reduction in the number of dollars received for each item by the exporter. Consider, for example, the

American oscilloscope manufacturer whose products are sold in France. If the dollar is worth 5 francs, a $400 oscilloscope would sell for 2000 francs. If a devaluation lowers the value of each dollar to 4 francs, then the exporter faces an attractive choice: he may either maintain the price of his product in francs, and receive a higher number of dollars ($500) in exchange; or he could maintain his export price in terms of dollars, and thus lower the price in francs (to 1600 francs) and reap increased sales. Typically, he will mix these two approaches, lowering his French price somewhat and gaining both in volume and in the dollar equivalent of the foreign price.

Since devaluation makes imports costlier in the United States, some American producers benefit from the reduction of competition: Bethlehem Steel has less to fear from Japanese steel mills. The loser is the American consumer, who must pay more for imported goods such as Fischer skis and often more for domestic goods sold in competition with the imports, such as Heads and Harts.

By the same logic, one reason Japan was able to sell so much in the United States before the revaluation of her yen was that the Japanese government maintained the currency at a low value. If Japan had accepted a higher value for the yen, her purchasing power abroad would have increased; but Sony sales abroad would have suffered. The long-standing undervaluation of the yen amounted to a huge exploitation of Japanese consumers, which was intended for the benefit of Japanese exporters, but incidentally conferred an annual gift of hundreds of millions of dollars on American consumers as well. Each $300 color television conveyed a $30 present (based on a comparison between Japan's old exchange rate and the new). Japan, by resisting for so long a change in the value of her money, and America, by demanding one, both placed protectionist politics ahead of national wealth. Of course, Japanese self-denial in the name of exports is hardly a problem that the United States need grapple with. If the Japanese choose to drain their resources to raise the American standard of living it is their hang-up, not ours. Or, as Milton Friedman has observed, "if Japan exports steel at artificially low prices, it is also exporting clean air. Why shouldn't we take it?"

Quite apart from protectionism, the Nixon Administration sought devaluation because it would produce a "strong" dollar and supposedly bolster American prestige. For years the United States resisted devaluation because she would betray the "weakness" of the dollar and therefore erode American prestige. In the night thoughts of the Kennedy Administration, devaluation played the same kind of role as "the fall of Southeast Asia"—an unthinkable foreign defeat that would spell political calamity at home.

In fact, there is no reason why national prestige should have anything at all to do with the exchange value of the dollar. Other nations have been able to strut about while maintaining overvalued rates, undervalued rates, multiple rates, or, as in Communist countries, no real exchange rates at all. Great Britain bravely held up the value of the pound in the 1920s and again in the 1960s, only to suffer from economic stagnation and uninterrupted international decline. De Gaulle's prestige was, if anything, enhanced by his swift devaluation of the franc after he took office in 1958.

But regardless of how little sense it makes to link our payments position with the national ego, the practice has both ancient and recent precedents. In the sixteenth and subsequent centuries, "mercantilist" ideologues and self-interested traders convinced statesmen that a nation's proper goal in trade was to import little, export much, and amass precious metals. England prospered, they thought, when it exchanged Lancashire wool for Spanish gold. In their view, gold was good, not because it could later be exchanged back for products, but simply because it was gold.

In this century, a more extreme version of this dogma has held sway. Countries strive with each other to amass international reserves even though these reserves now consist more of bookkeeping IOUs than of gold. Nations seek to maintain a balance-of-payments surplus—selling more abroad than they buy—so that their reserves will increase. Thus, for example, when De Gaulle's France devalued the franc, she traded away billions of francs worth of wine and Peugeots in return for a pile of gold and a sheaf of American IOUs in the form of dollars. France's aim was not to save up for a rainy decade but to impress her neighbors. The policy amounts to a kind of white man's potlatch, casting off goods in exchange for social prestige. The Nixon Administration's feverish enthusiasm for devaluation suggests that we, too, prefer the pleasures of the bankbook to those of the senses.

An even more discouraging motive for the Administration's decision to devalue was the perceived need to bow to the conventional morality of international finance. The United States is, and has been since the late 1950s, in substantial balance-of-payments deficit, amounting to $6 billion in 1969 and about $4 billion in 1970. What this means is simply that the amount we spend or send abroad for dashikis, vacations, investments, and wars exceeds the amount that foreigners are spending and investing in the United States. If it were only a matter of trade we would not have had a deficit at all until 1971. But military expenditures abroad ($4.8 billion in 1970) and heavy American investment in foreign industry have contributed to an unprecedented net outflow.

According to the banker's code that has governed thinking about international finance for over a century, all deficits are immoral and big deficits are unspeakably so. America, by this view, has an unqualified obligation to correct her deficit, regardless of the domestic sacrifices or foreign opposition that the necessary corrective steps would entail. Indeed, the measures invoked under the New Economic Policy to end the deficit—stopping gold redemption, imposing a tariff surcharge, demanding devaluation of the dollar—could be anticipated to injure American consumers and infuriate foreign governments. But they fulfilled our duty to the traditional dogma of financial orthodoxy which, as often in the past, triumphed over the real economic interests of its adherents.

The root of this tradition was the nineteenth-century exchange system based on the "gold standard." Payments for goods and investment abroad were transacted in gold as a matter of convenience. Since national money supplies were tied to gold coin (albeit loosely), countries that imported more than they exported automatically suffered the penalty of a reduction in the domestic supply of money. A nation's currency would literally end up abroad as a consequence of overly greedy importation of foreign goods.

The result, supposedly, was to reverse the flow of trade and restore balanced accounts without the government having to do anything at all. As money left the country, domestic prices were supposed to fall, making foreign goods relatively more expensive at home and domestic goods more attractive abroad. Moreover, the over-all economy would contract with the shortage of money. As business conditions worsened, demand for all goods—domestic and imported—would fall off. While this would create unemployment, it would also improve the balance of trade. Finally, the government might help the process along by raising the interest rate paid on bonds. High interest rates help the balance of payments by luring investments from abroad, but further deepen the decline in the domestic economy as it becomes harder for businesses to borrow for investment.

In sum, a country with a balance-of-payments deficit was supposed to endure some strong medicine—falling prices, rising interest rates, and plummeting employment—as the price for eliminating the deficit. The system did not work all that well, but most people viewed its harsh corrective mechanism as an inevitable punishment for the sin of financial irresponsibility.

A hybrid of this gold standard evolved over time. Dollars and pounds sterling became "reserve currencies." Both the Bank of England and the United States Federal Reserve Bank held large quantities of gold, and both were willing to exchange their currencies for gold at a fixed rate. It thus became the custom to hold reserves and settle international accounts in pounds or dollars as well as gold. This new status imposed special obligations on the United States and Britain to keep their currencies as good as gold. Under Chancellor of the Exchequer Winston Churchill, Britain restored the gold standard in 1925 to reaffirm her prewar financial preeminence.

But as John Maynard Keynes warned at the time, the reestablishment of the 1914 exchange value of the pound "amounts to an announcement that sterling *is* at parity with the dollar and will remain so. I suggest the right order of procedure is to establish the fact first and announce it afterwards, rather than make the announcement first and to chance the fact." Pessimistically, Keynes thought that Britain's economic managers would not in fact "chance" the maintenance of the pound's overvalued rate. Rather, he foretold, they would act to assure it through the restriction of credit and the deliberate intensification of unemployment.

And indeed they did. Keeping the British pound as good as gold became a symbol of national pride in England which successive governments during the 1920s supported at the price of a disastrous shortage of jobs. As one Liberal economist put it in 1931, the stability of sterling was "the one sheet anchor for Europe, and Britain the only country that could help Europe weather the storm." The British government's duty, thus perceived, was to cut the relief rolls, balance the budget, and calm the shattered nerves of continental bankers. Labour Prime Minister Ramsay MacDonald agreed, lost the bulk of Labour party supporters, and formed a coalition National Government to save the pound and thereby the country.

But the Depression forced Britain to abandon both gold and the habit of placing international propriety ahead of domestic needs. Later the United States followed suit. By going off the gold standard, Britain and the United States hoped to stimulate their own economies through export sales and protect domestic markets for local industries. They wished their own currencies to depreciate against the rest of the world's, making their goods cheaper and foreigners' more expensive.

But other countries retaliated with their own devaluations. As trade warfare grew more intense, countries erected tariff and quota barriers, instituted multiple exchange rates (Germany had Reisemarks for travel, Askimarks for trade with Latin America, Sperrmarks for blocked accounts, etc., each with a different value and different restrictions), and began making two-way barter deals instead of trading in world markets.

The low-tariff ideology of nineteenth-century liberalism waned along with its corollary, civilized bourgeois politics; in its place came a conception of exports and imports as tools of nationalistic rivalry, a kind of updated mercantilism. Germany, in particular, used bilateral trading to extract food and raw materials from central European nations, repaying them with inconvertible currency and surplus harmonicas. Countries of the British Commonwealth and Empire formed an informal monetary bloc, not consciously designed for political purposes but gratifying to Empire loyalists nonetheless. As the world economy split into insular trading cliques, trade diminished and the Depression intensified.

Little was learned from this experience except that international cooperation was needed to preserve exchange rates fixed in gold. At the end of World War II, the International Monetary Fund (IMF) was formed at Bretton Woods as a kind of business counterpart to the United Nations. A General Agreement on Tariffs and Trade (GATT) was signed, promising progress toward freer trade and lower tariffs.

The new system involved two modifications of the old one. To prevent the "beggar-thy-neighbor" policies of the 1930s, countries resolved not to use tariffs and other trade controls for balance-of-payments purposes. Measures such as the Administration's recent 10-per-cent import surcharge were flatly forbidden, on the theory that they would too readily provoke retaliation. The result was to tighten and codify the old rules of the game.

Countries in balance-of-payments difficulties were still expected to achieve equilibrium by shrinking their domestic economies and enduring unemployment in an effort to reduce imports. Only as a last resort were they supposed to alter exchange rates.

To cushion the impact of these rules, the IMF set up a short-term-loan fund to help countries that temporarily had deficits in their balance of payments. If, for example, France got into trouble in 1960, she could borrow up to $175 million (the amount of her contribution in gold to the Fund) with no questions asked. Further credit, up to a total of $800 million, could be available at the discretion of the IMF. The larger the amount of the loan, the more power the IMF would have to insist that France, in order to restore the balance, follow the "correct" fiscal and monetary policies that would tighten credit, slow down prices, and shrink the economy. These IMF loans represented the first creation of reserves by international agreement. Each member nation was pledged to accept IMF IOUs instead of gold or currency; but their amount was strictly limited and calculated in relation to gold. The result was a more resilient, though fundamentally unchanged, international exchange system.

In the pre-Bretton Woods negotiations on the world financial system, the British delegation (led by Keynes) had argued strongly for a system with greater resources and power. Keynes's proposed international clearing union would be empowered to create $30 to $35 billion in international reserves, of which a maximum of approximately $24 billion could have been used by debtor countries to purchase goods from the United States. Since the United States imagined a postwar world in which she would indefinitely be in balance-of-payments surplus (while the war-weakened European countries would chronically run up deficits), the Americans suspected that these credits would be put quickly to use by other countries. Hence, they feared the clearing union would simply be a mechanism for siphoning foreign aid from the United States, a joint bank account from which our cousins across the sea could help themselves to the fruits of American prosperity. As finally negotiated, the IMF provided for maximum drafts on the United States of $2.75 billion, barely over 10 per cent of Keynes's objective.

The British and the Americans also clashed over the new organization's power over creditor nations. Keynes argued for penalties to discourage any persistent payments imbalance, whether surplus or deficit (although, even with his plan, creditors would fare better than debtors). Again, the Americans resisted, picturing themselves in the role of a perpetual creditor being asked to take orders from foreign deadbeats. Once more the American argument (backed by cash and by the delegation's acknowledged sense of what Congress could be persuaded to accept) essentially won the day.

Keynes had feared that the new IMF, with its limited credit facilities and lack of authority over surplus nations, would prove inadequate to postwar trading needs. (He also commented that its charter was "written in Cherokee.") But while there was not much gold or IMF credit around to pay for European imports, during the late 1940s and early 1950s the gap was filled by enormous Marshall Plan aid from the United States. Later, private investment by Americans in Europe greased the wheels of exchange with dollars. The world's expanding needs for working capital were supplied, not by the IMF, but by American balance-of-payments deficits. The dollar became the world's chief "reserve currency";

countries would settle debts with other countries in dollars and hold the dollars as a reserve for their future needs.

As American deficits continued to mount, doubts were raised whether the huge amounts of U.S. dollars held abroad could be converted into gold. By 1960, foreign claims on the dollar amounted to $20 billion, while the American gold hoard was only $18 billion. The Kennedy Administration, obsessed with the nation's image abroad and committed to the restoration of pre-Sputnik American prestige, grew fearful of a run on Fort Knox. Maintaining a "sound dollar" and avoiding a currency crisis became high priorities for the government.

Two kinds of alternatives were available. On one hand, the Administration might limit domestic growth and employment for the sake of balance-of-payments rectitude. Tight-money policy would entice funds from abroad and encourage U.S. capital to stay at home, though it would also contract the domestic economy. A stringent budget policy, eschewing expansionary tax cuts and heavy government spending, would reduce our demand for imports—but only as a side effect of the general slowing down of business. These were the conventional measures that appealed to bankers and brokers. Within the Kennedy Administration they found their advocate in Treasury Secretary Dillon.

Schlesinger reports that a preinauguration task force, headed by George Ball, warned Kennedy that balance-of-payments problems "are being used in an attempt to frustrate expansionist programs at home and abroad and are giving aid and comfort to resurgent protectionism. So long as they remain unresolved, they may seriously hamper the freedom of action of your administration." Soon the prophecy came true. Progrowth policies for monetary expansion and increased federal spending had to be trimmed to meet the seemingly inexorable demands of the balance of payments. Even international politics sometimes felt the pinch of payments worries; Kennedy reportedly toyed with selling submarines to South Africa as a way of bringing in a little extra cash.

Had it not been for the Vietnam War, the American deficit would probably have soon disappeared, leaving the dollar "strong" but the world economy short of reserves. But as it happened, American military expenditures abroad and the booming, import-happy economy at home sent the deficit to new heights in the mid-1960s. Vietnam accounted for an $11-billion drain on the U.S. balance of payments from 1965 through 1968—$6 billion in direct military expenditures and $5 billion in extra imports and reduced exports resulting from the fact that the economy was being run at a faster tempo during the war than Congressional conservatism had ever permitted during peacetime. In addition, direct investment abroad by U.S. corporations exceeded foreign companies' investments in the United States by $8 billion during the same period. Thus, the United States would probably have had a substantial payments surplus if she had either stayed out of Vietnam or severely constricted corporate investment overseas.

The Johnson Administration, of course, did neither. It did extend some of its predecessor's policies, adding some new controls on capital outflow. In 1965, it imposed a series of "voluntary" restraints on long-term lending by banks to foreigners, with the clear hint that failure of voluntary action would provoke strict controls. But for the most part the Johnson Administration chose to ignore the balance of payments. Its own objectives, Vietnam escalation and home-

The Balance of Payments: The Cross of Gold   167

front prosperity, took precedence over its fear of international financial embarrassment.

The result was the long-expected "crisis" on gold convertibility. Speculators and merchants rushed to dump their dollars for gold, and in March 1968, the world's central banks had to suspend their gold payments to private parties. America still remained pledged to redeem a foreign government's dollar holdings with gold, but this clearly had become a *Catch*-22 promise, valid only until put to a real test. Any substantial run on the dollar would have forced the United States to stop converting dollars to gold.

The crisis came and went, leaving the United States with a continuing deficit, billions owed in foreign debts, and the most prosperous economy in its history. The United States imposed new controls on foreign investment by American corporations, but otherwise continued business as usual. Soon, economists and officials began to wonder whether the situation was really as perilous—or immoral—as orthodox economists suggested. Theorists began formulating a "benign neglect" policy toward the balance of payments. The United States, they argued, had no special responsibility to stanch her payments flow. Other nations, if they wished, could move to reverse their accumulation of dollars. They could pass laws to restrict new American investment, or they could raise the value of their currencies, thus discouraging exports to the United States and encouraging imports. But if they failed to do these things, America need not slow down her economy, or sacrifice her national programs, for the sake of international good citizenship.

This policy became influential in the Nixon Administration; but to the Europeans, it represented the summit of arrogance. Heedless of balance-of-payments constraints, America had financed the foreign-currency needs of her military expansion in Asia and corporate expansion in both Europe and Asia (e.g., in Korea) simply by spending dollars and letting others accumulate them. Because of the dollar's role as an international reserve currency, the Europeans complained, there was no effective limit on this process. Americans could buy abroad with overvalued dollars and expect foreign governments to hoard these pieces of paper, as if international finance were a giant Monopoly game, with the United States as banker. Without ever having asserted the right—and certainly without having been granted it—the United States had managed to get an indefinite free ride from the world's other trading nations.

A special source of grievance for many Europeans was the use of America's deficit to finance her investments in European industry. "Fifteen years from now," wrote Jean-Jacques Servan-Schreiber in the late 1960s, "it is quite possible that the world's third greatest industrial power, just after the United States and Russia, will not be Europe, but *American industry in Europe.*" Between 1964 and 1970, American investment in Europe totaled $21 billion.

The European complaint against our "benign neglect" policy had merit, as far as it went. Had Europe shown any interest in stemming the flow of dollars by revising exchange rates, the United States would have had some moral obligation to cooperate. Indeed, we would have had little choice. Since the United States did not have enough gold to redeem the dollars held abroad, the Europeans could at any time have forced us to abandon the parity and let the dollar "float" to a new, lower level. But, in fact, the European governments, like the Japanese, kow-towed to their exporters and resisted devaluation of the dollar. The Japanese govern-

The Balance of Payments: The Cross of Gold 169

ment blithely presented the United States with an annual offering of underpriced television sets and cameras, while Germany contributed cheap binoculars, and France subsidized Chanel. In these countries auto, steel, textile, and other manufacturers of exports wield even more power than their counterparts do in the United States.

At first blush, it would seem politically easier for the European governments to stem the influx of American investment dollars into their banks and industries. But Continental Europe's relatively expensive and undeveloped credit markets are inadequate to serve the needs of European business. American loans have provided a source of cheap, ample credit to firms whose expansion plans would otherwise have been trimmed to the dimensions of local lending. Even when Americans were buying shares in local companies or setting up their own subsidiaries, rather than simply lending money, the European attitude has been ambivalent. De Gaulle warned against a Europe "colonized by foreign participations, inventions and capabilities," and a Common Market manufacturers' association whined about American companies which were "often 'misinformed' about price structures existing in European markets." Americans, their EEC competitors claimed, "tended to provoke price wars." But it was precisely the American firms' challenge to Europe's high-priced cartel that endeared them to the technocratic guardians of the Common Market's antitrust policy. More importantly, European governments saw American corporate investment as the source of new jobs and new technology. General Electric was allowed to buy up the shares of Machines Bull in the hope of infusing American expertise into the floundering French computer industry. Finally, rivalry among the European nations precluded any common front against American investment. As French Premier Michel Debré observed in 1959, "If U.S. firms are going to set up plants in the Common Market, it is better, under any circumstances, that they choose France rather than her partners." Only in Japan, where the market for debt finance is highly developed and the giant trusts can generate their own funds for new investment, has local business been united on keeping the Americans out. In sum, America's vast payments deficit persisted not simply because America found it convenient to continue spending dollars, but because her trading partners were not adverse to receiving them.

Similarly, if the Europeans had proposed a revamping of the world monetary system to eliminate the privileged reserve status of the dollar, we would have had little right to object. Our *de facto* ability to make unlimited purchases of goods with dollars could not be defended in principle. But as it happens, it was the United States that pushed proposals to increase the amount of international reserves that are not tied to the dollar, and the Europeans who have dragged their feet.

For years the French had their own proposal: to topple the almighty dollar by restoring the reign of gold as the major world reserve currency. But this could hardly be called a reform. Raising the exchange value of gold would temporarily increase world reserves—each nation's gold stock would be worth more in goods and national currencies —but it would have no impact at all on the basic problem of allowing countries to solve payment imbalances without crippling their domestic economies. In effect, increasing the price of gold would transfer the American reserve privilege to the major owners of gold—Middle Eastern sheiks, European speculators, and South African businessmen.

In view of the European attitude, the American attempt to force devaluation made little sense as an act of international duty. It might be defended as a stratagem for forcing the issue of broader monetary reform, anticipating the eventual collapse of the dollar standard, and taking the initiative in changing it. But the motives behind the New Economic Policy were only in part so sanely strategic. Campaigning for the demise of the dollar standard was largely an act of devotion, reinforcing the tradition that national prosperity and autonomy should be sacrificed to bankers' ideology.

National autonomy, of course, is not always put to worthy uses. The dollar's privileged position in world finance has made it easier to fuel the war in Vietnam. Stringent adherence to the orthodox rules would have limited our power to achieve all of our objectives, including the most deplorable ones. But it was not military adventures that the Nixon Administration intended to jettison—rather, it was the threat to special interests and conventional wisdom posed by the continued acceptance of inexpensive foreign goods.

Mercantilist measures and speeches followed closely on the announcement of the New Economic Policy. Treasury Secretary John Connally predicted that America's loss of world markets might lead to a deteriorating standard of living and, eventually, "a revolution in this country." To stave off revolution, Connally proposed a "transformation" in business-government relations, chiefly through the means of export subsidies and new antitrust exemptions. "Hell," he observed, "compare what we do here for American business interests to what Japan does."

Meanwhile, Congress approved an Administration tax scheme—the Domestic International Sales Corporation— best summarized in the headline to an advertisement by a

Wall Street bank: "Now American exporters can help the government by not paying all their income taxes." Anyone with $2500 in capital can set up a new export corporation. So long as all its assets are devoted to exporting, it can "defer" up to half of its income-tax liabilities. These deferred taxes can be used to make a loan to the export corporation's parent company—in effect, plowing the tax deferral back into the business. The net result is a $170-million-per-year tax cut for exporters.

Balance-of-payments anxieties also helped generate interest in a far more significant tax proposal—the adoption of a national value-added tax (see Chapter 2). Under the trading rules agreed upon in the GATT, "direct" taxes on business —such as a sales tax or the VAT—may be rebated to exporters. "Indirect" business taxes, such as the corporate income tax, may not. The DISC probably violates these rules, but so do many nations' export-promotion schemes. Rather than flirt with further illegality, so the argument goes, the United States would be best off slashing the corporate income tax and substituting a heavy VAT. The tax could then be legally rebated, and American exports would gain a competitive advantage.

Tax gimmicks such as DISC and VAT rebates amount to a concealed devaluation of the dollar. Instead of directly cheapening the price of American goods to foreigners—by openly reducing the value of the dollar—these measures accomplish the same result under camouflage. In the process they distort the U.S. tax system. Their supposed balance-of-payments "benefits" are benefits only on the assumption that it is always in America's interest to increase exports—a mercantilist delusion.

But notwithstanding these protectionist gestures, the results of the New Economic Policy may well turn out to be superior to its intentions. The monetary agreement of November 1971, inevitably hailed by President Nixon as "the most significant . . . in the history of the world," was by itself no giant step for mankind. The dollar was depreciated by 12 per cent, an expected result, even if one which we had little reason so feverishly to seek. More importantly, gold convertibility was not restored, and U.S. negotiators insisted that it would not be. The obligation to pay out gold for dollars had for years symbolized the rigidity and irrationality of the international monetary system; in James Tobin's words, "Much of the evolution of money through the centuries has been its progressive liberation from its traditional dependence on precious metals, a wasteful and often pernicious constraint on the ability of men to manage their own affairs." With gold fading from the picture, a start could be made on designing a more rational world monetary system.

The most obvious reform plan is also the most venerable —a proposal to increase the size of international reserves by giving the IMF more power to create credit on its own. But even its sponsors recognize that reserve creation does not cure chronic balance-of-payments problems. New reserves alone would not prevent the speculative currency raids and international financial confrontations of recent years. A country which persistently spends more than it earns abroad will eventually run short of reserves; only the United States has been able consistently to play the debtor, and that was because the dollar is itself the major medium of international reserves. Germany or England could not go on a buying binge without eventually running out of gold, dollars, and IMF borrowing power. At that point, something would have to give. If the dollar eventually loses its reserve status, we will be in that position, too. The debtor must, as Eisenhower said, find a way to pay his bills.

Under the Bretton Woods regime of fixed exchange rates, the chronic debtor's lot is not an easy one. Two effective methods of improving its balance are banned by international agreement: a country may not raise tariffs or let its exchange rates fluctuate in the market. (The U.S. 10-per-cent surcharge and the "float" of European currencies were both deviations from the rules.) Another alternative, restricting foreign investment, is considered legal but not quite cricket: only in 1968, with the dollar in extremis, was America expected to impose comprehensive controls. Thus a nation shy on reserves must take one of two paths to equilibrium: it can "tighten its belt" by reining in the entire economy in order to curb the demand for imports, or it may raise interest rates to lure and hold capital. If it wishes to avoid these harsh purgatives, it must brave the displeasure of the international banking community and choose the path of devaluation.

In theory, devaluation is not so painful. With exports cheaper and imports more dear, the country sells more and buys less from abroad. However, labor unions, fearing lower living standards, may push up wages and thus inflate export prices. Consumers can accelerate their spending to maintain the same level of imports. Speculators, conscious of these events, may resume pressure on the exchange rate. In most cases, there will eventually be a balance-of-payments gain from devaluation; but for a year or two turmoil may persist.

While the balance-of-payments gain from devaluation is delayed, the political losses are often immediate. Devaluation can be a blatant token of political failure, and its promoters risk the fate of Harold Wilson's Labour government, whose fortunes ebbed with the pound. Sometimes, to be sure, these dangers are exaggerated. For years, American Administrations were terrified of the electoral consequences of a change in the value of the dollar. As it turned out, "nobody gives a damn"—to quote the president of a major U.S. shoe manufacturer, who, if anyone, should care about devaluation. The American economy is too big, and import prices are too inconsequential, for exchange rates to matter much. Smooth talking by the President can portray the devaluation as an international victory rather than a defeat—if anyone gives a damn about that either.

Perhaps Nixon's successful venture will make devaluation easier for American Presidents. But other countries, more dependent on imports or more sensitive to international opinion, still find devaluation traumatic. Harold Wilson's troubles stemmed in part from his own emotional commitment to the pound, but his countrymen, too, were conditioned.

With devaluation so tricky and domestic measures so unpleasant, attention has turned to Milton Friedman's radical suggestion for abolishing the government's adjustment problem altogether. Friedman would let exchange rates among currencies float freely according to the pressures of the market. If, one year, American beer-drinkers all switched to Heineken's or American tourists decided to discover Europe first, dollars would glut the market and our exchange rate would drop. American goods would become cheaper to foreigners, just as in a formal devaluation, and eventually the exchange rate would stabilize.

Supporters make out a powerful case for floating exchange rates. Governments, they say, would no longer be committed to maintaining their exchange rate and would have no obligation to seek balance-of-payments harmony. Domestic

monetary and fiscal policy could proceed with relative freedom from international complications. An American government that wanted to reduce unemployment could pump
up the economy without great worry about the trade accounts. As imports rose, the dollar would indeed fall—but
without a crisis or an international confrontation. Floating
exchange rates certainly would not be an answer to all of
our economic problems, but they would give the government greater leeway to pursue an aggressive growth policy.
For this reason, more flexibility in international exchange
has long been advocated by many economic scholars.

Traditionalist European bankers, and some economists,
dispute this view. Floating exchange rates, they warn, are a
gate-pass to anarchy. Speculators who now dally with stocks,
bonds, and cocoa beans would switch their bets to foreign
exchange. The yen and the mark might become "growth currencies," and the British pound could fluctuate with merger
rumors.

The world's limited experience with floating exchange
rates does suggest the perils of speculation. In the early
1920s, speculative capital inflows buoyed the pound to its
pre-World War I levels, encouraging the British government
to make its disastrous 1925 decision to restore fixed rates at
the old parity of $4.87 to the pound. Once committed to the
prewar exchange rate, the British government had to improve its trade balance by imposing deflation and unemployment. Britain was thus forced to endure a decade of stagnation even prior to the world Depression. Here the fault
must be shared between the floating rate system which gave
the false signal in 1925 that the old parity was still valid, and
the fixed system which perpetuated the error. If Britain had
continued with floating rates, the capital flow eventually

would have reversed itself and the pound would have slid to a lower and more appropriate level.

The more recent Canadian experience makes a stronger point for the skeptics. In the late 1950s, huge capital flows pushed the flexible Canadian dollar up to U.S. $1.09. The government decided to coax the rate downward and speculators overreacted. The rate was finally fixed at $.925, well below the level the government had wanted. The lesson may be that governments are never indifferent to their nations' exchange rates. If countries have conflicting balance-of-payments goals, as they often do, a regime of floating rates might be an invitation to exchange-rate warfare. And aside from such extraordinary threats, flexible rates put a burden on normal trade. They raise the cost of insurance against exchange loss and introduce new uncertainties into investment decisions.

These costs are, however, probably minor compared to the huge toll taken by the orthodox prescription for balance-of-payments adjustment. Throughout most of the 1950s and early 1960s and again in 1971 and 1972, the "full-employment gap"—the lost output due to unemployment of men and machines—exceeded the *total* amount of U.S. overseas exports or imports. At worst, the uncertainty created by floating rates might impose a cost on the economy equal to 1 or 2 per cent of the value of trade—half a billion to a billion dollars, a sum which sounds large in the abstract but which is small potatoes in our trillion-dollar economy.

For a while after the August 15 measures it seemed possible that the international monetary system might peacefully convert to floating exchange rates. With America no longer supporting the dollar, its rate would automatically float unless other countries chose to prop it up by dumping their currencies for a yet greater accumulation of dollars. But that is precisely what Japan and France did. In one day the Japanese government purchased more than one billion dollars by selling yen at the old exchange rate. France allowed floating rates for certain purposes but tried to maintain the old fixed rates for imports and exports. Economists called these measures a "dirty float"—a regime of ostensibly floating rates in which governments were still trying to manipulate the market to assure fixed parities.

Bloated with dollars, the Japanese and the Europeans eventually gave up their defense of their old exchange rates. But they insisted that the new ones be fixed, not floating. For the time being, at least, the balance of payments would be the same old game, with a different set of handicaps.

Only recently has the economics profession come to grips with the fact that the balance of payments is essentially a political problem. This realization is at the root of the approach developed by Richard N. Cooper, a Yale economist and former White House adviser. Cooper argues that the postwar movement toward freer trade and investment has had a serious and little-recognized price. Increasing economic integration among countries means that any one nation's economy is becoming more vulnerable to changes in another's. With money moving across the Atlantic at the flick of a Telex switch, minor changes in American interest rates have immediate repercussions in the Dutch bond market. Demand for autos in Berkeley helps determine employment at Wolfsberg's Volkswagenwerke.

The misunderstandings and exchange crises of recent years, Cooper suggests, are a natural consequence of the fact that the fast pace of economic integration has not been matched by political unification. Just as the original American colonies imposed tariffs and restrictions on each other's exports before these were prohibited by a common Constitution, so do today's nation-states wage war in the money markets in the absence of a world government. Since there is no sovereign Parliament or Super-Diet embracing Japan, Europe, and the United States, disagreement about trade flows or exchange rates makes itself felt through a kind of chaotic competition.

In the long run, Cooper suggests, the answer lies in greater political integration. But its pace cannot be forced. We are not yet ready to give Italy an official voice in our budget policy, and vice versa. For the while, the best strategy is to control the pace of economic integration to minimize destructive competition. Increasing the flexibility of exchange rates would best allow countries to pursue independent economic policies. But if exchange-rate flexibility is not allowed, Cooper argues that the alternative need not be contrived recessions. Instead of requiring this perverse adherence to the "rules of the game," Cooper would allow countries to interfere with free trade and capital movements for balance-of-payments purposes. To guard against protectionist abuse, these restraints would be subject to international rules. Across-the-board tariff surcharges or capital-export taxes might be permitted, while discriminatory controls on particular products or countries would not.

Cooper does not advocate this step toward economic isolation as a permanent solution, but rather as an interim compromise until the challenges of political interdependence are met. One danger of this approach may be the difficulty of reversing a psychology of self-defense. A President might find it difficult to dismantle "temporary" restraints imposed on foreign transactions. The newly revived protectionist clique may not self-destruct on cue from the White House.

Even Cooper's plan requires a measure of international agreement and rationality—both scarce commodities. For this reason there is something to be said for one proposal which requires no international agreement at all. It is a game which only one nation can play well—the United States—but its attractions for us are substantial.

The notion is simple. The United States unilaterally sets a value for the dollar, meanwhile announcing that she has no intention of defending that value against speculative attack or balance-of-payments deterioration. If other countries wish to prop up the dollar, that's their business. Otherwise, we are content to let it float. Such a policy would, with one blow, break the yoke of balance-of-payments orthodoxy and leave policy-makers free to get on with the real task— managing domestic prosperity.

The disadvantages of benign neglect are political. American nonchalance would be perceived not so much as the *Realpolitik* of a nation with more important problems to work out, but as a rejection of international cooperation. Europe could, albeit irrationally, prefer the construction of retaliatory tariff barriers to simple revaluation against the inconvertible dollar.

The likely European reaction reflects the ambiguity of attitudes toward the United States that has long prevailed in international financial circles. The sheer volume of American trade is so great and the convenience of banking in New York instead of Paris or Rome is so indispensable that the United States has always held the trump card in financial negotiations. But Washington's lack of understanding of its own power, combined with the force of conventional bankers' wisdom, has often left the United States in the position of supplicant. We could always have maintained the position that the balance-of-payments problem is not ours but theirs. We get the goods; they get the paper. The Europeans and Japanese have always been in a position to solve it, but have preferred to transfer the psychological burden to the "guilty" party.

A few central ideas emerge from the murky political economy of international finance. Trade is unimportant in the United States in relation to domestic prosperity. Yet a mixture of stupidity, misplaced internationalism, and private venality has often allowed balance-of-payments considerations to be placed ahead of other national goals. Any system which permits policy-makers to assert the priority of domestic prosperity is better than any system that relies on the discipline of unemployment and slow growth. Conventionally, the virtues of one reform plan over another have been judged on how well each facilitates international trade and finance. After all, trade—as David Ricardo pointed out ages ago—is a good thing. French champagne is better than the New York State variety. But the gains from trade, and the facilitative benefits of reform, pall in importance beside the benefits of exorcising the nineteenth-century ethics of the gold standard.

Epilogue

Growth for the sake of growth is the ideology of the cancer cell.

—Earth Day Poster

I've been poor and I've been rich and, believe me, rich is better.

—TALLULAH BANKHEAD

At the depth of the Great Depression, John Maynard Keynes wrote an essay entitled "Economic Possibilities for Our Grandchildren," sketching the potential of a century of continued economic growth. "I draw the conclusion," Keynes said, "that assuming no important wars and no important increase in population, the economic problem may be solved or be at least within sight of solution, within a hundred years." By the "economic problem" Keynes meant the struggle for subsistence, "the primary, most pressing problem of the human race." Someday it would disappear.

I see us free, therefore, to return to some of the most sure and certain principles of religion and traditional virtue—that avarice is a vice, that the exaction of usury is a misdemeanour and the love of money is detestable, that those walk most truly in the paths of virtue and sane wisdom who take least thought for the morrow. We shall once more value ends above means and prefer the good to the useful. We shall honour those who can teach us to pluck the hour and the day virtuously and well, the delightful people who are capable of taking direct enjoyment in things, the lilies of the field who toil not, neither do they spin.

But beware, the time for all this is not yet. For at least another hundred years must we pretend to ourselves and to everyone that fair is foul and foul is fair; for foul is useful and fair is not. Avarice and usury and precaution must be our gods for a little longer still. For only they can lead us out of the tunnel of economic necessity into daylight.

Forty years have passed; wars and population growth have retarded the dawn of affluence for hundreds of millions— while those who have gained the means for leisure have not thereby become like lilies of the field.

Keynes foresaw the problem: "To those who sweat for their daily bread, leisure is a longed-for sweet—until they get it. . . . There is no country and no people, I think, who can look forward to the age of leisure and abundance without a dread."

That many of us have reached that age, and experienced that dread, goes far to explain our new qualms about growth. "Work and living have become more and more pointless and empty," writes Charles Reich. "Our life activities have become plastic, vicarious, and false to our genuine needs." The work ethic is waning, but no satisfactory play ethic has come to take its place. Those of us who toil not are far too likely to spin.

This malaise is real, and tragic, and it serves as a reminder of the imperfect connection between money and happiness. We have not meant to assert otherwise.

Thus far, we have made use of a simple argument to answer the critics of growth. Growth has had disagreeable side effects, we have admitted, but these can best be attacked head-on. Economic abstinence is too harsh a remedy and often an inadequate one.

But if zero growth is not a cure-all, neither is rapid growth. For the $17,000-a-year professor or the $80,000 radiologist, life's problems may not be significantly reduced by added income. As more and more Americans reach advanced levels of affluence, the role of money in their lives will inevitably diminish and may in fact become perverse. We have no illusion that man lives by electric toasters alone.

All we argue is that the most favored few per cent in our society should not project their attitudes on those less materially fortunate. Suffocating leisure is not the danger facing the fender man at the Ford Dearborn plant who takes home $162.86 for forty hours on the assembly line, and probably does overtime when he can get the work. Nor does it terrify the New Jersey Bell Telephone operator who answers hundreds of information calls a day and must hurry through a drugstore lunch. A two-hour, paid lunch break or a $20 raise would be unlikely to break her spirit or send her careening into group therapy.

Parenthetically, we question whether even the affluent could not receive a genuine and worthy pleasure out of increased income. Professor Galbraith skis regularly in Gstaad, and he finds it a salubrious hideaway from the telephone and a convenient location from which to write compositions on the evils of private consumption. It is an expensive pleasure but obviously a productive one. We see no reason to deny it indefinitely to others.

Source Notes

Index

Source Notes

PAGE

INTRODUCTION: THE RETREAT FROM RICHES

3. John Kenneth Galbraith, *The Affluent Society* (Boston: Houghton Mifflin, 1958), p. 1.
3. Ezra J. Mishan, cited by Wade Greene and Soma Golden, "Luddites were not all wrong," *The New York Times Magazine*, November 21, 1971.
5. Ezra J. Mishan, *The Costs of Economic Growth* (Harmondsworth, Middlesex: Penguin Books, 1967), pp. 179–80.
10. Anthony Lewis, *The New York Times*, January 28, 1972.

I. OBJECTIONS TO GROWTH AS A GOAL

Chapter 1. Fouling the Nest

19. Loren Eiseley, quoted in Richard Neuhaus, *In Defense of People* (New York: Macmillan, 1971), pp. 126–27.
19. Captain Donaldson, quoted in Henry Jarrett, *Environmental Quality in a Growing Economy* (Baltimore: Johns Hopkins University Press, 1966), p. vii.
19.–20. Richard Neuhaus, *op. cit.*, p. 71.
20. *Honolulu Daily Advertiser*, cited by Francine du Plessix Gray, "Profiles—Hawaii (II)," *The New Yorker* (March 11, 1972), p. 72.
21. On plastic packaging, see Barry Commoner, *The Closing Circle* (New York: Knopf, 1971), p. 128.
22. On known mineral supplies exhausted within one hundred years see U.S. Council on Environmental Quality, *First Annual Report* (Washington, D.C.: Government Printing Office, 1970), p. 158.
23. On fish catches, see Charles L. Schultze *et al.*, *Setting National Priorities: the 1973 Budget* (Washington, D.C.: Brookings Institution, 1972), p. 377.
24. On atmospheric temperature, see *Man's Impact on the Global Environment: Assessment and Recommendations for Action,*

Carroll L. Wilson and William H. Matthews, eds. (Cambridge, Mass.: M.I.T. Press, 1970), Chapter 1.

24. On SST effects, see Commoner, *op. cit.*, p. 31.

25. On fertilizer runoffs, see Barbara Ward and René Dubos, *Only One Earth* (New York: W. W. Norton, 1972), p. 69.

25. On Aswan dam, see Commoner, *op. cit.*, p. 184.

25.–26. Anthony Lewis, *The New York Times,* January 30, 1972.

26.–27. "Disaster Lobby" comment by Thomas R. Shepard, Jr., cited in Commoner, *op. cit.*, p. 10.

27. Dennis L. Meadows, *et. al.*, *The Limits to Growth* (New York: Universe Books, 1972).

30. Meadows, *ibid.*, p. 23.

31. John Ise, "The Theory of Value as Applied to Natural Resources," *American Economic Review* (June 1925).

31. President's Materials Policy Commission, *Resources for Freedom,* Vol. I (Washington, D.C.: Government Printing Office, 1952).

32. Man-hours, Harold J. Barnett and Chandler Morse, *Scarcity and Growth: The Economics of Natural Resource Availability* (Baltimore: Johns Hopkins Press, 1963), p. 206.

33. On fusion-reactor development, the corporation is KMS Fusion, a division of KMS Industries, Ann Arbor, Mich.

34.–35. *Man's Impact on the Global Environment, op. cit.*

36. Garrett Hardin formula, quoted in Neuhaus, *op. cit.*, p. 186.

36. Commoner, *op. cit.*, p. 128.

36. Union Camp slogan, quoted in James M. Fallows, *The Water Lords: Ralph Nader's Study Group Report on Industry and Environmental Crisis in Savannah, Georgia* (New York: Grossman, 1971), p. 81.

36.–37. Union Camp officials quoted in *ibid.*, pp. 92, 113.

37. Wallace quoted by Marshall Frady in *Harper's Magazine* (May 1970), cited in Fallows, *op. cit.*, p. 128.

37.–38. Commoner, *op. cit.*, pp. 258, 261.

38.–39. Garrett de Bell, ed., *The Environmental Handbook* (New York: Ballantine, 1970), quoted in Dirck Van Sickle, *The Ecological Citizen: Pollution Survival and Activist's Handbook* (New York: Harper & Row, 1971) p. 200.

39. "Day-old bread," etc., in *ibid.*, p. 174.

40. Ford letter quoted in John C. Esposito, *Vanishing Air: Ralph Nader's Study Group Report on Air Pollution* (New York: Grossman, 1970), p. 37.

40. Auto air-pollution suit, see Mark J. Green with Beverly C. Moore, Jr., and Bruce Wasserstein, *The Closed Enterprise System: Ralph Nader's Study Group Report on Antitrust Enforcement* (New York: Grossman, 1972), pp. 254–64.

41. David Zwick and Marcy Benstock, *Water Wasteland: Ralph*

Nader's Study Group Report on Water Pollution (New York: Grossman, 1971), p. 406.

41. Cost estimates on 100-per-cent versus 97-per-cent waste removal are from testimony of Paul McCracken, then chairman of the Council of Economic Advisers, using Council on Environmental Quality figures; cited in *National Journal*, February 22, 1972.

41.–42. Marc Roberts, "Public Policy for Water Pollution Control," paper presented to the Council for Policy Evaluation, 1972, and his "Who Will Pay for Cleaner Power?" paper prepared for the Sierra Club Conference on Electric Power Policy, 1971. The arguments here are drawn from those papers and his "River Basin Authorities: A National Solution to Water Pollution," *Harvard Law Review*, May 1970.

42. $316-billion estimate, Council on Environmental Quality estimate, cited in *National Journal*, February 22, 1972.

42.–43. Robert N. Grosse, "Some Problems in Economic Analysis of Environmental Policy Choices," in U.S. Department of Health, Education, and Welfare, Public Health Service, Consumer Protection and Environmental Health Service, *Proceedings of Symposium on Human Ecology* (Public Health Service publication No. 1929. Washington, D.C.: Government Printing Office, 1969), p. 48, as cited in Tax Foundation, Inc., *Pollution Control: Perspectives on the Government Role* (New York, 1971), p. 40.

42.–43. Delaware estuary study, cited in Council on Environmental Quality, *Environmental Quality (Second Annual Report, 1971)* (Washington, D.C.: Government Printing Office, 1971), p. 121.

43. Beet-sugar plants, in *ibid.*, p. 118.

43. Over-all cost estimates for water-pollution abatement, cited in *National Journal*, February 22, 1971.

44. GAO study, "Examination into the Effectiveness of the Construction Grant Program for Abating, Controlling and Preventing Water Pollution," Report to the Congress by the Comptroller General of the United States (U.S. General Accounting Office, Nov. 3, 1969). See also Schultze *et al.*, *Setting National Priorities: the 1972 Budget*, Chap. 12, and *Setting National Priorities: the 1973 Budget*, Chap. 11.

44. On tax incentives, see Marc Roberts, "River Basin Authorities: A National Solution to Water Pollution," and Stanley Surrey, "Federal Income Tax Reform: The Varied Approaches Necessary to Replace Tax Expenditures with Direct Governmental Assistance," *Harvard Law Review*, December 1970.

45. Marc Roberts, "Public Policy for Water Pollution Control," p. 7.

45. On jackhammer noise, *Environmental Quality, Second Annual Report*, p. 102.

46. On Con Ed stations, see Neil Fabricant and Robert M. Hallman,

Toward a Rational Power Policy: Energy, Politics, Pollution (New York: Braziller, 1971), p. 23.
47. On electric heating and cooling, in *ibid.*, p. 78.
48. On direct fossil-fuel conversion, in *ibid.*, p. 82.
48. London air cleanup, Wilfred Beckerman, "Economic Development and the Environment: A False Dilemma," *International Conciliation*, January 1972.
48. Cost estimates for high standards of air and water quality, Schultze, *et al., Setting National Priorities: the 1973 Budget*, p. 375.
49. Claude Julien, America's Empire (New York: Pantheon, 1971), p. 23.
49. V. I. Lenin, *Imperialism, the Highest Stage of Capitalism* (Peking: Foreign Language Press, 1965), p. 9.
53.-54. Smedley D. Butler, cited in John Gunther, *Inside South America* (New York: Pocket Books, 1968), p. 161.
54. Raymond Vernon, *Sovereignty at Bay* (New York: Basic Books, 1971).
57.-58. Guano story from Jonathan Levin, *The Export Economies* (Cambridge, Mass.: Harvard University Press, 1960).
58.-59. On Liberia-Firestone relations, see Wayne C. Taylor, *The Firestone Operations in Liberia* (Washington, D.C.: National Planning Association, 1956).
59. "Impracticable," cited in *ibid.*, p. 76.

Chapter 2. Sharing the Wealth:
Income Redistribution as an Alternative to Growth

61. Frederick Lewis Allen, *The Big Change* (New York: Harper, 1952), p. 286.
62.-63. Arthur M. Schlesinger, Jr., *The Vital Center* (Boston: Houghton Mifflin, 1949), pp. 159, 153.
63. Distribution statistics from S. M. Miller and Pamela Roby, *The Future of Inequality* (New York: Basic Books, 1970), p. 38.
63.-64. John Kenneth Galbraith, *The Affluent Society* (Boston: Houghton Mifflin, 1958).
64. John Kenneth Galbraith, *The Liberal Hour* (Boston: Houghton Mifflin, 1960), p. 21.
64. Unless otherwise identified, the references in this chapter to the history of liberal redistributive programs in the United States are derived from *Congress and the Nation, 1945–1964* (Washington, D.C.: Congressional Quarterly Service, 1965).
67. Leonard Chazen, "Participation of the Poor: Section 202(a)(3) Organizations under the Economic Opportunity Act of 1964," *Yale Law Journal*, March 1966.
72. On relative income of nonwhites and whites, see J. Gwartney,

"Changes in the Non-White/White Income Ratio, 1939–67," *American Economic Review,* December 1970.

72. The discussion here of tax deductions, tax incentives, and tax expenditures largely summarizes two *Harvard Law Review* articles by Stanley Surrey: "Tax Incentives as a Device for Implementing Government Policy: A Comparison with Direct Government Expenditures" (February 1970) and "Federal Income Tax Reform: The Varied Approaches Necessary to Replace Tax Expenditures with Direct Governmental Assistance" (December 1970).

74. Tax benefits are calculated from figures in Joseph A. Pechman and Benjamin A. Okner, *Individual Income Tax Erosion by Income Classes* (Washington, D.C.: Brookings Institution, 1972). The estimate for the budget subsidy for low- and middle-income housing is for fiscal year 1972 and is taken from Charles L. Schultze *et al., Setting National Priorities: the 1972 Budget* (Washington, D.C.: Brookings Institution, 1971), p. 278. See also the excellent study by Henry Aaron, *Shelter and Subsidies: Who Benefits from Housing Programs?* (Washington, D.C.: Brookings Institution, 1972).

75. On the Kaiser committee, see *A Decent Home, Report of the President's Committee on Urban Housing* (Washington, D.C.: Government Printing Office, 1969).

75. George Romney quote in *The New York Times,* March 28, 1972.

76. On tax rates, see Pechman and Okner, *op. cit.*

77. On the redistributive effect of state and federal tax systems, see Joseph A. Pechman, "The Rich, the Poor and the Taxes They Pay," *The Public Interest,* November 1969; Tax Foundation, Inc., *Tax Burdens and Benefits of Government Expenditures by Income Class* (New York, 1967).

78. On higher education, see W. Lee Hansen and Burton A. Weisbrod, *Benefits, Costs and Finance of Public Higher Education* (Chicago: Markham Publishing Co., 1969). See also the comment by Joseph A. Pechman, "The Distributional Effects of Public Higher Education in California," in *Journal of Human Resources,* Vol. 3, p. 361. Using the Hansen-Weisbrod data, Pechman shows that the average lower-middle-income family was a net beneficiary of higher-education spending, while the average family earning above $25,000 paid a net subsidy. The results follow from the fact that California's tax system, while regressive (i.e., taxing higher incomes at lower *percentage* rates than low and medium incomes), still levies higher dollar amounts of tax on the upper-income groups.

78.–79. On the Education Bank, see James Tobin, "Raising the Incomes of the Poor," in Kermit Gordon, ed., *Agenda for the Nation*

(Garden City, New York: Doubleday, 1968), p. 92; James Tobin and Leonard Ross, "A National Youth Endowment," *The New Republic,* May 3, 1969.

80. On farm subsidies, see Charles L. Schultze, *The Distribution of Farm Subsidies: Who Gets the Benefits* (Washington, D.C.: Brookings Institution, 1971).

80. Budget figures are from Schultze, *et al., Setting National Priorities: the 1972 Budget.*

81. Arthur M. Schlesinger, Jr., *The Crisis of Confidence: Ideas, Power and Violence in America* (Boston: Houghton Mifflin, 1969), p. 248.

81. On the assumption that there had been redistribution, see Enoch Powell, *Saving in a Free Society* (London. Hutchinson, 1960); Bertrand de Jouvenel, *The Ethics of Redistribution* (New York: Cambridge University Press, 1952).

82. C. A. R. Crosland, *The Future of Socialism* (London: Jonathan Cape, 1956).

82.–84. On trends in income distribution in Britain, the work by Richard Titmuss and his associates at the London School of Economics has discredited the myth that Labour accomplished an egalitarian revolution. See Richard Titmuss, *Income Distribution and Social Change* (London: George Allen & Unwin, 1962). A recent study by Adrian Webb and Jack E. B. Sieve (*Income Redistribution and the Welfare State,* [London: G. Bell & Sons, 1971]) confirms and extends Titmuss's argument: British welfare-state benefits were financed largely by regressive taxation. Government taxes have been simply proportional to income and thus not redistributive; and, although government benefits have differentially helped low-income groups, the effect has been significant only for the poorest categories. In some fields, government programs designed for the poor have come to benefit the nonpoor even more. In 1962, for example, 29 per cent of heads of households in council dwellings (public housing) had incomes over £650 a year, while only 24 per cent of private tenants had this income.

Nor has the private economy become more even-handed. Webb and Sieve conclude that *"the estimated inequality of final income remained constant over a period of twenty years (1939–1959) which saw the establishment and growth to some maturity of the 'welfare state.' "*

On the Wilson Government's record, see Peter Townsend, "The Problems of Social Growth," *The Times* (London), March 8–11, 1971.

In America the myth of increasing equality was first systematically challenged by Gabriel Kolko, *Wealth and Power in America* (New York: Praeger, 1962).

84. Nicholas Kaldor, *An Expenditure Tax* (1945), p. 242, cited in Titmuss, *op. cit.*, p. 196.
86. Figures for fiscal year 1972 from Schultze *et al.*, *Setting National Priorities: the 1972 Budget*, p. 187.
87. D. P. Moynihan, cited by Robert Goodman, *After the Planners* (New York: Simon & Schuster, 1971), p. 166.

II. OBJECTIONS TO THE
ECONOMIC SIDE EFFECTS OF GROWTH

Chapter 3. The New Economics and the
Old Shibboleths: A Short History

95. George Humphrey, quoted in Herbert Stein, *The Fiscal Revolution in America* (Chicago: University of Chicago Press, 1969), p. 295.
95. Eisenhower, quoted in Congressional Quarterly Service, *Federal Economic Policy* (Washington, D.C.: Congressional Quarterly Service, 1969), p. 35.
98. John Kenneth Galbraith, *The Affluent Society* (Boston: Houghton Mifflin, 1958), p. 253.
99. Sherman Adams, *Firsthand Report* (New York: Harper & Brothers, 1961), p. 155.
100. Eisenhower remark to reporters, quoted in *ibid.*, p. 171.
101. On Eisenhower and Humphrey, see Marquis Childs, *Eisenhower: Captive Hero* (New York: Harcourt, Brace, 1958), pp. 248–49.
101. Chamber of Commerce of the United States, *Economic Lessons of Postwar Recessions: Report of the Committee on Economic Policy* (Washington, D.C., 1959).
101. Eisenhower on Baruch, quoted in Stein, *op. cit.*, p. 336.
102. Yntema, quoted in *ibid.*, p. 338.
102. Humphrey, quoted in Adams, *op. cit.*, p. 382.
103. Charles E. Silberman, "What Happened in the U.S. Economy," in Richard E. Mulcahy, *Readings in Economics from Fortune Magazine* (New York: Holt, Rinehart and Winston, 1967), p. 194.
103. Stans, quoted in *ibid.*, p. 194.
104. Nixon, quoted in Stein, *op. cit.*, p. 370.
104. Wallich, quoted in Silberman, *op. cit.*, p. 196.
108. Kennedy, quoted in Theodore C. Sorensen, *Kennedy* (New York: Harper & Row, 1965), p. 408.
108. Kennedy, quoted in Stein, *op. cit.*, p. 405.
110. Arthur M. Okun, *The Political Economy of Prosperity* (Washington, D.C.: Brookings Institution, 1970), p. 50.
111. Kennedy, quoted by Sorensen, *op. cit.*, p. 409.

111. James Tobin, *National Economic Policy* (New Haven: Yale University Press, 1966), p. 160.

111. Arthur M. Schlesinger, Jr., *A Thousand Days: John F. Kennedy in the White House* (Greenwich, Conn.: Fawcett, 1965), p. 601.

112. Roosa, quoted in Gilbert Burch, "The Balance of Payments Bind," in Mulcahy, *op. cit.*, p. 290.

113. Okun, quoted in *Newsweek,* January 24, 1972.

115. Okun, *The Political Economy of Prosperity,* p. 42.

Chapter 4. The Perils of Inflation

117. Supermarket manager, quoted in a seminar paper by Joel Wachs, Columbia University School of Law, May 1972.

117.–118. John Kenneth Galbraith, *American Capitalism: The Concept of Countervailing Power* (Boston: Houghton Mifflin, 1952), p. 198.

118. Dwight D. Eisenhower, speech of June 8, 1959, quoted in Stein, *op. cit.,* p. 354.

127. C. E. Metcalf and J. D. Mooney, "Aggregate Demand Model," unpublished working paper for the Office of Economic Opportunity, 1965, cited in R. G. Hollister and J. L. Palmer, *The Impact of Inflation on the Poor* (Institute for Research on Poverty discussion paper, University of Wisconsin, 1969).

128. George Bach and Alfred Ando, "The Redistributive Effects of Inflation," *Review of Economics and Statistics,* February 1957.

129. On inflation compressing wage differences, see Arthur M. Okun, Henry M. Fowler, and Milton Gilbert, *Inflation: The Problems It Creates and the Policies It Requires* (New York: New York University Press, 1970), p. 16 and source cited.

137. On innovation and firm size, see Frederic M. Scherer, *Industrial Market Structure and Economic Performance* (Chicago: Rand-McNally, 1970), p. 361.

137. On lone inventors, see John Jewkes, David Sawers, and Richard Stillerman, *The Sources of Invention* (New York: St. Martin's Press, 1959).

138. Peter McColough, quoted in Sanford Rose, "U.S. Foreign Trade: There's No Need to Panic," *Fortune,* August 1971, p. 110.

138. Henry Ford II, quoted in *The New York Times,* August 23, 1971.

139.–140. Letter of Richard Olney to President Perkins of the Chicago, Burlington and Quincy Railroad, December 28, 1892, quoted in Marver H. Bernstein, *Regulating Business by Independent Commission* (Princeton: Princeton University Press, 1955), p. 255.

140. On air fares, see Michael Levine, "Is Air Regulation Necessary? California Air Transportation and National Regulatory Policy," *Yale Law Journal,* 1965.

146.–147. On Korean controls, see Tobin, *op. cit.*, pp. 117–18.

148. IRS official, quoted in *The New York Times,* March 12, 1972.

Chapter 5. The Balance of Payments: The Cross of Gold

151. Paul A. Samuelson, quoted in W. Carl Biven, *Economics and Public Policy* (Columbus, Ohio: C. E. Merrill, 1966), p. 89.

151. Schlesinger, *A Thousand Days,* p. 601.

152. Eisenhower, at a March 4, 1959, press conference, quoted in Stein, *op. cit.*, p. 352.

155. Meany, quoted in Rose, *op. cit.*, p. 111.

155. Gott, quoted in *ibid.*, p. 110.

158. Friedman, quoted in *ibid.*, p. 111.

161.–162. John Maynard Keynes, *Essays in Persuasion* (New York: W. W. Norton, 1963), p. 231.

162. "Sheet anchor," Walter Layton, reporting from Geneva, "the alarm of continental bankers," quoted in Robert Skidelsky, *Politicians and the Slump: The Labour Government of 1929–1931* (Harmondsworth, Middlesex: Penguin Books, 1967), p. 391.

162.–163. On multiple exchange rates, etc., see Charles P. Kindleberger, *International Economics* (Homewood, Illinois: Richard D. Irwin, 1963), p. 297.

166. Schlesinger, *A Thousand Days,* p. 599.

167. On balance-of-payments effect of Vietnam War, see Leonard Dudley and Peter Passell, "U.S. Balance of Payments and the War in Vietnam," *Review of Economics and Statistics,* November 1968.

169. Jean-Jacques Servan-Schreiber, *The American Challenge* (Harmondsworth, Middlesex: Penguin Books, 1969), p. 17. Italics in original.

170. De Gaulle, quoted in Charles P. Kindleberger, *American Business Abroad* (New Haven: Yale University Press, 1968), p. 78.

170. Common Market manufacturers association, statement of the Union des Industries de la Communauté Européene, quoted in *The New York Times,* March 15, 1967, cited in Kindleberger, *American Business Abroad,* p. 78.

172. Connally, quoted in *The Wall Street Journal,* April 24, 1972.

179.–180. See Richard N. Cooper, *The Economics of Interdependence.*

EPILOGUE

183.–184. John Maynard Keynes. "Economic Possibilities for Our Grandchildren," reprinted in Keynes, *Essays in Persuasion* (New York: W. W. Norton, 1963).

184. See Charles Reich, *The Greening of America* (New York: Bantam Books), pp. 6–7.

Index